SOCIOLOGY FOR OPTIMISTS

To Stevi Jackson, Lynn Jamieson, Sue Scott, Liz Stanley and Catherine (Lane) West-Newman. Many people have helped me through the sociological world, but these women have been outstanding in their encouragement over the years and I thank them.

SOCIOLOGY FOR OPTIMISTS

MARY HOLMES

Los Angeles | London | New Delhi
Singapore | Washington DC | Melbourne

Los Angeles | London | New Delhi
Singapore | Washington DC | Melbourne

SAGE Publications Ltd
1 Oliver's Yard
55 City Road
London EC1Y 1SP

SAGE Publications Inc.
2455 Teller Road
Thousand Oaks, California 91320

SAGE Publications India Pvt Ltd
B 1/I 1 Mohan Cooperative Industrial Area
Mathura Road
New Delhi 110 044

SAGE Publications Asia-Pacific Pte Ltd
3 Church Street
#10-04 Samsung Hub
Singapore 049483

Editor: Chris Rojek
Editorial assistant: Delayna Spencer
Production editor: Katherine Haw
Copyeditor: Kate Campbell
Indexer: Martin Hargreaves
Marketing manager: Michael Ainsley
Cover design: Jen Crisp
Typeset by: C&M Digitals (P) Ltd, Chennai, India
Printed and bound by CPI Group (UK) Ltd, Croydon, CR0 4YY

© Mary Holmes 2016

First published 2016

Library of Congress Control Number: 2016933340

British Library Cataloguing in Publication data

A catalogue record for this book is available from the British Library

ISBN 978-1-4462-6867-4
ISBN 978-1-4462-6868-1 (pbk)

CONTENTS

ABOUT THE AUTHOR

Mary Holmes is a sociologist at the University of Edinburgh. Her research is in the areas of the sociology of emotion, intimacy and relationships and political sociology. She has taught sociology in Scotland, Australia and New Zealand. Her recent books include *Distance Relationships: Intimacy and Emotions Amongst Academics and their Partners In Dual-Locations* (Palgrave Macmillan, 2014) and *Heterosexuality in Theory and Practice* (with Chris Beasley and Heather Brook, Routledge, 2012).

PREFACE

This book is the work of a partial, prejudiced and ignorant sociologist.[1] It struck me many times in writing it that it was hubris to attempt such a wide-ranging yet short account of the state of sociology as a discipline. I cannot quite recall how the idea for the book came about, except to say that I have long wondered whether and why sociology is intrinsically a miserable social science? Such wondering was prompted partly by a regular phenomenon, familiar to many who teach sociology, of students informing me that I had 'ruined' some aspect of their life. Having learned some sociology they now could not watch a movie/go on holiday/read a magazine/talk to their family/buy clothes or do anything much without analysing it in ways not usually conducive to enjoyment or peace of mind. Yet in telling me this they were not always sorry, and recognised gain as well as loss. Sociology provides valuable alternative understandings of the world. It can tell us things we do not hear from politicians or journalists; it makes us question how we live and how we do things and it points out the flaws of our societies. However, on other occasions my students, myself and many of my colleagues feel a frustration with critical sociological analysis of the terrible state of the world and want to know what can be done. If there is anything of value in this work, I hope it might encourage sociologists and students of sociology to take stock of what they have to offer for making sense of the world in which we live, and for changing it.

Gradually it became clear to me that I wanted to advocate sociology as a way of thinking which not only criticises what is wrong with society, but which critically imagines how it could be otherwise – including 'better'. Sceptical as sociologists have been when I have explained the book to them, they have also encouraged me by saying they think there is a need for it. I hope so. I have certainly been accused of being an optimist, sometimes with the implication that to be so is an intellectual failing or a regrettable personal foible. Optimism previously referred to the philosophical doctrine that this world is divinely created and thus the best of all possible worlds (Leibniz 1952/1710: 118). Now it typically means an individual psychological attitude involving 'a tendency to hold positive expectations of the future' (Bennett 2011: 303, see also 301). As I will set out, I understand optimism not as a failing, not as disposition, but as a critical action of the will (Gramsci 1973/1929: 175). It takes effort to exercise critical optimism, but I argue that it is vital in order to better interpret and change the world. Certainly it is important to try.

In spirit the book also owes much to C. Wright Mills's (1959) book *The Sociological Imagination*. I have not sought to reproduce that classic, but have been inspired by the way that Mills wrote. He wrote a short, readable book intended for students, but also of interest to colleagues. He wrote for students in ways that assumed they were intelligent human beings. He advocated for a particular approach to sociology, promoting it not as a science but as an imaginative way of thinking about the world. There are plenty of big sociology textbooks on the market containing glossy pictures and coverage of a wide range of sociological debates. Like Mills, I have aimed more towards a simple book that advocates a way of doing sociology: an optimistic way. I assume that students can and will read these essay-like chapters. Indeed I hope the students reading this might learn about essay writing by looking at how the chapters are written. The book may not always be easy, but I hope it has things that you can enjoy and that you will persevere even if you sometimes find it difficult. Pushing through those difficulties is a crucial part of learning and learning can be enjoyed.

As I set out to explain why optimism is important to sociology I am slightly worried that I stole the idea behind this book from my friend Chris Beasley. She and Heather Brook and I talked for some time about writing about Pollyanna Politics and I honestly cannot remember whether my desire to write about optimism in sociology preceded this or not. This is to acknowledge a truly collegiate relationship and friendship with these two women and to humbly beg their forgiveness for not being able to untangle my own ideas from our collective musings. The book would be better if they had written it with me, but I stubbornly went on without them and they supported me, as always.

While I was developing the ideas for the book I had the opportunity of teaching many of the ideas behind *Sociology for Optimists* as a Masterclass to fourth year honours students at Flinders University in Adelaide. I want to thank those who were students in the class for giving me insights into their own work and helping me think anew about sociology as a discipline. They also helped me think about optimism in sociology from a range of different angles and I hope this has enriched the book. The students in the class were Meredith Barrett, Ferdinando Biroccesi, Nathan Dalton, Damien Day, Michelle Esterhuizen, Brett Lennox, Samuel Muscat, Konstans Ostreva, Steven Renfrey, Andrew Riley and Zoei Sutton. (Catherine) Lane West-Newman came over from the University of Auckland to contribute to teaching the class and was a fount of intellectual inspiration. There were also appearances by my colleagues Riaz Hassan and Eduardo de la Fuente, I thank them for their collegiate respect. Doctoral students at the time: Jordan McKenzie, Dani Clark and Erin Carlisle also engaged with some sessions and impressed me as always with their fine minds. This class helped me consider some of the problems of my project but also made me very optimistic about the future of sociology.

The book you write is never quite the book you imagined, but if it gets anywhere near it is because of all those who helped. Norman Stockman was very kind and absolutely brilliant in the feedback he gave me on two chapters. His theoretical and disciplinary knowledge is awe inspiring. Those chapters no longer exist, but appear in different parts of the book, I hope making it better. Thank you to Nathan Manning, who read and helped improve an early version of what is now the chapter on freedom. The encouragement means a lot. Isabelle Darmon saved me from embarrassing misinterpretations of Marx and Weber in the Nature chapter, provided helpful references and quietly suggested jaw-droppingly good ideas, which I at once tried to appropriate without having the wit to do them justice. Anonymous readers Sage organised were also hugely helpful. Brent always helps and even though I was not entirely delighted when he telephoned me while I was trying to write what I thought was the final sentence of the book, of course he managed to inspire me as always.

I am also indebted to numerous sociological colleagues for listening to me complain about the book. My sociology colleagues at the University of Edinburgh, have been kind, respectful and yet rigorously insightful in their critical engagement with these ideas. Their interest in the project has helped refine what it is I am trying to say here and why it might be important to say it. Appalling as much that happens in that world is, to me the point of sociology is that there is nothing inevitable about the way social life is organised. It could be otherwise and that means it could be 'better'. Discussions of what 'better' might mean and how it might be achieved are crucial. Sociology has much to offer these discussions and I hope this account of the need for critical optimism can be a small part of that offering.

What we can see or hear from a sociological perspective is necessarily limited (Kemple and Mawani 2009: 231), but lack of optimism imposes particular kinds of blinkers. In pessimistic terms, the emergence of sociology is usually talked of in terms of European thinkers making sense of the evils of industrialisation, and it is right that more should be understood about how sociology was implicated in

eugenics, imperialism and the destruction of other peoples and worlds
it involved (Connell 2007; Kemple and Mawani 2009; Renwick 2012).
More attention to this is needed, but this book makes rather uneven
efforts in that direction. I do try to draw on ideas and examples beyond
Europe (including the UK), USA, Canada and Australia. Other limitations to sociology may have shifted and this needs noting. It may be the
case that by the mid-twentieth century the social conditions in which
sociology was done produced either a short-sighted abstracted empiricism or a rather blurred grand theoretical vision (Mills 1959). Now it
may be grand empiricism and abstracted theorising that are dominant
and equally problematic in how they depoliticise sociological thinking, restrict its communication to a wider world and limit the utility
of sociology for addressing social problems (Kemple and Mawani 2009:
234–5). Yet, if the world is sometimes one of possibilities and not just
problems, then sociology must try to understand those possibilities. It is
important to consider imperialism not just as the destruction or subjec-
tion of passive 'others' (Tuhiwai-Smith 1999), nor just to put yourself
in the shoes of others, as Mills (1959) recommends. It is important to
listen (Back 2007), to learn to see the rest of the world from other perspectives (see, for example, Connell 2007). To centre the periphery and
peripheralise the centre. This applies both to the world and to sociology.

If you look at most big introductory sociology textbooks, once they
have dealt with explaining what sociology is, they will cover roughly the
same list of topics: gender, race and ethnicity, class, crime and deviance,
education, work and organisations, the media, health and illness, families, religion, urban life, politics, the state. Occasionally there might be a
chapter on poverty or on inequality or the environment or globalisation.
None of these topics inherently require a pessimistic stance, but this hard-
centred version of the sociological selection box typically presents these
topics as ones that are fundamentally about continuing social inequalities, the control exercised by social institutions like work, family and the
media and the increasing power of governments over their citizens. Thus,
I depart from such a representation of the discipline in this book.

The book is organised so as to show how a sociology for optimists
might help us see the world in a slightly different way. The first chapter
deals with how society is reproduced and how it changes. The focus is
on social institutions like families, education and the media, but also on
the importance of friends. Here an optimistic stance can allow exploration of how privilege is maintained, but also how it is challenged.
Chapter 2 uses critical optimism to understand how people might find
ways to enjoy their lives, and find pleasure even where social conditions
might seem to make that difficult. The examples are about leisure,

work and sex. Not only hope for more enjoyment but optimistic orientation towards greater freedom should be considered. Thus Chapter 3 discusses social and pro-democracy movements, organised crime, 'swinging' (swapping sexual partners), and youth culture as forms of resistance to social constraints. In further evaluating what a 'better' society looks like, it is argued in Chapter 4 that a critically optimistic sociology must deal with morals and ethics. Optimistic expectations for greater social equality are important in furthering these ethical evaluations and so that is taken up in Chapter 5. Emerging from these discussions is the importance of the relationship of individuals to those around them and the continued force of such connections is explored in Chapter 6. Trends around marriage, fertility and ways of living are examined from an optimistic stance. Chapter 7 then considers the insights to be gained from optimistically rethinking the relationship between human beings, other animals and nature; insights vital to dealing with challenges such as climate change. This leads to the reflections in Chapter 8 on forms of enchantment within current societies, and on how sociologists can optimistically consider the social importance of beliefs, meaning and imagination. The final chapter discusses to what extent sociology has involved optimism, and what we can learn about the necessity of some form of optimism for thinking sociologically. I maintain that sociologists and sociology are stronger when optimism is part of our critical repertoire.

Mary Holmes
Edinburgh, November 2015

Note

1. I paraphrase Jane Austen's description of herself as author of the *History of England*, which she wrote aged 15. See the British Library's virtual copy of the manuscript at www.bl.uk/onlinegallery/ttp/austen/accessible/pages1and2.html#content.

1

CHANGE

When I started high school in 1979, my fairly average state-run New Zealand school had one computer. It was nothing now recognisable as a computer, it was an old, heavy TV set which one of the maths teachers would rig up to something called a card-reader. We learned to write simple computer programmes, marked them on special cards with a black felt-tip pen and fed them into the card reader and watched the fuzzy numbers and letters on the screen to see if the programme worked. By the time I left high school five years later, the school had a whole room full of 'personal computers' much more like the ones around now. Primitive forms of email allowing communication between some machines emerged and less than ten years later I was looking at one of the first browsers and learning to surf the internet. Now I can type this paragraph on my phone or tablet and send it to anyone, upload it to a social network site or to the cloud. Then I can make a video phone call to almost anywhere in the world using the same device. These quite rapid technological changes have had a huge impact on how we live our lives, how we interact and communicate, how we learn, and how we spend our time. These changes are just one example of change in the social world that has taken place over the last one to two hundred years. Part of what sociology is about is trying to make sense of these changes and how they relate to other aspects of social life that do not seem to change so much, but instead are reproduced from one generation to the next.

If optimism is about expectation of a better future, then a sociology for optimists needs to understand how change occurs. There is a tension in sociology between understanding how society is reproduced much as it is and how it changes, although the two intersect. This entails questions about whether reproduction describes the continuance of inequalities and whether change is allied to progress or improvement. Social institutions are regarded as central in social reproduction, although they also experience change. Institutions are patterned sets of practices that continue over time; with families being considered especially important, I discuss these changes in detail in the chapter on relationships (Chapter 6). Other major institutions are education and the media. Peers or friends are not institutions but also play key roles in maintaining the social world and yet can also allow for change. Institutions also often pass on privilege, so that the groups who are wealthy and have status continue to benefit from the way that society is organised. However, change does occur, including within these institutions as people instigate, participate in and resist change. This chapter charts some of the key social changes of the last century or so in order to assess whether change is something to be (critically) optimistic about.

Changing Education

An optimistic view of change needs to think critically about what socialisation processes teach us. These processes contain the first learning experiences people have as children learn the rules and norms of their society, learning not only how to walk and talk but how to walk, talk, eat, sleep, go to the toilet, and so on, 'properly'. Elias (1991) argues that this means learning to regulate their behaviour by controlling their bodies to fit with social norms. He points out that as societies become more complex, the time it takes to prepare children for adulthood lengthens (Elias 1991: 29–30). Children learn initially from their parents, who are significant others, as George Mead (1962) would call them, but they also learn as they start to make sense of themselves and their parents in terms of the wider society in which they live. It is a highly classed, gendered and culturally specific process (Bourdieu 1987; Oakley 1972). Children and young adults go on being socialised 'in specialised institutes, schools and universities' (Elias 1991: 29).

As they grow older, children learn about social expectations and are able to take the perspective not only of significant others but of the generalised other (Mead 1962). They learn what people in general, what the wider society, expects of them. Parents socialise children in keeping with a range of social expectations. Within Functionalism – a sociological approach that emphasises what useful purpose our social arrangements serve, these socialisation processes have been understood as contributing to social stability or the reproduction of society in a similar form to the past. For example, Parsons and Bales (1956) argued that women and men were socialised into supposedly complimentary expressive and instrumental roles within families. They claimed that men learnt to be goal oriented and competitive, while women learnt to be nurturing and emotionally expressive, at least in mid-twentieth century America. This, they claimed, usefully divided labour within a complex society. The asymmetrical power relations and related disadvantages attached to women's expressive role were not considered (Hochschild 1973).

Socialisation theories, even less Functionalist ones, were heavily focused on mothers, blaming them and assuming children passively take on norms and expectations. Yet, such norms and expectations are often unclear and even contradictory, and critical thinking is not well served by simply dismissing those who are different as somehow having failed to be socialised properly (Stanley and Wise 1983). Families are not total institutions (Goffman 1968), they do not control every aspect of their members' lives like in a prison, and thus important as the role of parents may be in socialising children, mothers and fathers and children exist in a social world, where children learn how to be from a variety of sources and have to make some decisions in navigating their way through the world (Stanley and Wise 1983; Thorne 1993). This means exercising some agency.

To appreciate how positive change, not just the reproduction of inequalities, can be enabled by learning, some appreciation of reflexive agency is required. Reflexivity describes how people reflect on their lives and use that knowledge to shape their lives; agency refers to any kind of capacity to do that shaping. By inadequately accounting for reflexivity, much sociology is pessimistic about how difference and inequalities are reproduced by socialisation of children within families (see, for example, Bourdieu 1987; Oakley 1972). Pierre Bourdieu (1987) for instance, argues that class inequalities are reproduced via processes of distinction; an idea very similar to socialisation theories about the social 'training' of children by their parents or carers. For Bourdieu, the habitus – the embodied practices that are learned within the family – are powerful in sedimenting inequalities. He proposes that 'taste classifies and it classifies the classifier' (Bourdieu 1987: 6). His argument is that people use their learned, class-based likes and dislikes for cultural and material products to mark themselves out as different from those in other classes. It is, however, the tastes of the middle classes that are dominant in these processes and their higher social status allows them to reinforce the idea that their taste is good, and those of classes below inferior. Distinction as a reproducer of hierarchies fosters disrespect of those without the 'proper' habitus, which is not just classed but gendered and 'raced' (Bourdieu 1987; Skeggs 1997).

The way that habitus operates at a fundamental embodied level and is, as the word indicates, deeply habitual rather than conscious, makes it very hard to change. Thus, although this framework recognises that people can learn a new habitus, as with socialisation theory it cannot easily explain how or why someone may come to escape the ingrained habitus of their early years. Bourdieu's view of structure is that it is relatively unchanging and that social positions produce dispositions and those dispositions reproduce social positions. Margaret Archer (2007; 1993), however, believes that habitus has limited value as a concept in the early twenty-first century because we cannot rely on intergenerational socialisation. Rather a more calculating form of reflexivity is needed, requiring knowledge that previous generations cannot pass on, for example digital competency. Bourdieu fundamentally under-estimates the degree to which people must now deal with new situations, although routine action still has a place and habit may play more of a part in reflexivity than Archer suggests (Elder-Vass 2007). At the very least, reflexivity is not always highly conscious or cognitive, but involves emotions, bodies and relating to others (Holmes 2010). Thus, despite the emotional stickiness of structural inequalities (Ahmed 2004), people move and are moved towards change.

Change certainly seems evident within education as an institution, as it has 'improved' in the sense of schooling becoming less elitist and more inclusive, especially for women. In the past formal education was reserved for the more privileged members of society, and mostly for the men. As Virginia Woolf (1986/1938) explains in the 1930s about education in England:

> All educated families from the thirteenth century to the present moment have paid money into that account [for the education of their sons]. It is a voracious receptacle. Where there were many sons to educate it required a great effort on the part of the family to keep it full. ... And to this your sisters, as Mary Kingsley[1] indicates, made their contribution. Not only did their own education, save for such small sums as paid the German teacher, go into it; but many of those luxuries and trimmings which are, after all, an essential part of education – travel, society, solitude, a lodging apart from the family house – they were paid into it too. (p. 7)

Access to further education has slowly improved. From the late nineteenth century onwards, compulsory primary school education was introduced in Britain, most American states, Canada, Australia and New Zealand and expansion of some kind of schooling occurred in many other countries.

In countries still largely based around agriculture or manufacturing goods, governments did not feel the need to encourage more than fairly basic learning which would not upset current divisions of labour, but enable workers to better fulfil their tasks, which as technology became more complex might require some degree of literacy and numeracy (Benavot and Riddle 1988). More extensive education has remained limited to a small, if increasing minority. By the mid-twentieth century only a tiny proportion of people, even in the wealthiest countries only about 3 per cent of adults, are estimated to have completed tertiary education. However, by 2010 around 8 per cent of those over 15 had completed university in 'advanced' countries and almost 6 per cent in developing nations (compared to 0.5 per cent in 1950). Although a significant increase, it hardly seems radical, but it indicates that improvements have occurred that do extend more education to more people.

One improvement is the reduction of the disparity that existed between average years of schooling for girls and boys, especially in developing countries. In 1950 girls in those countries were at school around 62 per cent of the years boys were at school, but by 2010 they had 86 per cent of the amount of schooling boys had. By 2006 there was gender parity in primary and secondary school enrolments in 59 of 176 of the countries reporting, up from only 39 countries in 1999 (Charles 2011: 358). Globally, the proportion of women enrolled in secondary education has continued to increase, reaching around 60 per cent in 2007, only just behind men. This reflects the improvement in the percentage of women enrolled in secondary education in less developed countries, where just over 50 per cent of women as well as of men were enrolled by 2007 (United Nations Statistics Division 2010). However, girls are likely to have, on average, one year less schooling than boys in developing nations and half a year less in 'advanced' nations (Barro and Lee 2013). Yet, almost equal proportions of girls and boys are now receiving the highest A-level grades in England. This may be due to changes in the subjects girls are taking, but they remain under-represented in science and maths (Department of Education 2014: 7–8). Across subjects, however, in 2012/13 around 56 per cent of university undergraduate students in the UK were women, and women undergraduates in the UK are equally likely as men to obtain a first class degree (Higher Education Statistics Agency 2014). Both women's enrolment rates and university level achievements have shown a substantial increase across the world, with only 27 per cent of tertiary students being women in 1965, whereas women have been making up 50 per cent or more of the world's undergraduates since 1990 (Charles 2011: 358). In America, women at university level have outnumbered men since the late 1980s and since the beginning of this century have usually obtained around 57 per cent of bachelors' degrees, while the percentage of masters and doctoral degrees they earned also increased, albeit this percentage is much lower, 20 per cent or less, in Maths and Engineering, showing the uneven nature of improvements for women (England 2010: 160; US Department of Education 2013). Other relatively wealthy countries, such as Japan, have seen massive increases in women going to university, although they still form a slightly lower percentage of students than men. Meanwhile there is some variance in the majority world. Gender differences are fairly small in Latin America. India, however, has a somewhat smaller proportion (40 per cent) of women than men in tertiary education, but has seen an impressive rise in their enrolment since the 1950s. By contrast, Mongolia has had more women than men in higher education since the 1970s, a relatively common situation in East Asia (Charles 2011: 358; Nozaki et al. 2009). While there may be problems measuring women's educational participation and success relative to men, all these measures do indicate that many more women than in the past are able to get an education and to achieve within the education system up to the highest levels.

Meanwhile, there has also been a significant, if less dramatic, widening participation of working class people in higher education since the 1990s. Around one quarter of students accepted to university in the UK in 2005 came from the four lowest socio-economic groups, although this proportion has not always continued to rise since then and is lower at more elite universities. Similar class inequalities persist in the USA (Reay et al. 2010: 107–8). However, a shift from 5 per cent of young people enrolling in UK higher education in 1950 to 35 per cent in 2007, is not trivial, and this expansion is similar in other wealthy nations (Boliver 2011: 231). It is significant enough to warrant new forms of sociological explanation that can better explain such positive change.

A critically optimistic lens must renew sociological debates around education in order to account for changes, as the reproduction of inequalities seems less complete than in the past. Education no longer simply operates to reproduce class by making workers' children into workers and managers' children into managers. Pierre Bourdieu and Jean Passeron (1977) outlined in detail how this did happen in the twentieth century as the school system privileged and rewarded the kinds of knowledge – the cultural capital – that middle class children already had and working class children often did not. Despite Bourdieu's (see also 1987) radical criticisms of class privilege, his model makes changes in the system seem unlikely, only occurring if a working class individual can somehow learn the 'right' kind of knowledge to allow them to join the middle classes. This does not suggest how class as a system of privilege might be challenged or alter, nor how working class children may reject the middle class nature of schools. Those like Paul Willis (1977), who did explore such rejection amongst working class boys in England, concluded that it ensured failure and did not encourage change. Middle class children (although he focused on boys) learned the skills they needed to manage others, while working class children were taught to be obedient and disciplined; they were 'learning to labour'. By misbehaving and not valuing school work, the boys were asserting a stereotype of working class masculinity and contributing to the reproduction of their lower place in the class hierarchy (see Connell et al. 1982 for a similar argument about Australian education). Sue Sharpe (1976) similarly saw schools as reproducing gender inequalities by promoting ideologies of women as naturally suited to caring roles and men to 'important' paid work, and by reinforcing economic and historical forces shaping gender. Like Willis, Sharpe sought to understand how even if children resisted what they were being taught, they tended to accept some of these ideas in ways that actually reproduced inequalities. How, then, was the opening up of education described above able to happen?

Accounts of education have become more optimistic in seeing the possibility of diverse kinds of resistance less linked to class and gender (Furlong et al. 2011: 363), partly by understanding reproduction and change as linked. For example, Barrie Thorne's (1993) study of elementary school children in America credits them with some agency in navigating the different, sometimes conflicting, gender expectations coming from the school and their peers. They have to do gender differently as they move between the spaces of the classroom and the playground. Nevertheless, Thorne does not see this as meaning that children are free to choose how to be girls or boys, but she highlights the way in which children may police gender in the playground in ways that reinforce hierarchies in which boys reign (see also Prendergast and Forrest, 1998). Reproduction is not the opposite of change, as although gender hierarchies may continue, Thorne can help in seeing how they also are more open and shifting as children interpret and enact gender divisions in a variety of ways and in ways which alter in different contexts and are different from the past. Such approaches can appreciate how, from the 1980s, partly as a result of deliberate changes in schools, girls caught up with and overtook boys in terms of academic success. This sparked concern over the 'failure' of boys (Cortis and Newmarch, 2000; Mac an Ghaill, 1994), but change is also possible for boys, especially if educators pay attention to boys' own ways of constructing academically successful forms of masculinity (Skelton and Francis 2011). Also to say that girls were more likely to achieve better results, did not necessarily mean that boys were 'failing'. These measures of girls' versus boys' success are part of the neoliberal emphasis on school and teacher effectiveness that can mask the more complex intersection of gender with class, ethnic and other forms of inequality in school life. Such auditing may also fail to appreciate less easily measured forms of learning that may be valuable to young people (Connell 2011: 58–72; Ringrose 2007). Overall, a focus on problematic measures of success at school is at best useful because it may help challenge prejudices about the intellectual inferiority of girls and because exam success is key in securing entry to tertiary education. However, people's experiences of tertiary education and its outcomes have altered.

The concept of social generations may also be useful in forging critically optimistic explanations of how what it means to go to university has changed and differs for different social groups such as different classes and genders. A generation is a set of people who share 'historically specific material conditions' and ways of making sense of the world (Furlong et al. 2011: 361). The notion of generations overcomes past divisions between cultural and structural explanations of young people's lives. It means thinking about culture – meaning young people's own understandings and identities – but relating these to the social conditions or structures in which those cultural meanings exist. For example, the expansion in tertiary education from the 1990s, especially in the UK, has not guaranteed that the more diverse graduates produced all enter middle class careers, as happened in the past. It is argued that mass education made post-secondary education less elitist but established new hierarchies, with some institutions and types of courses having more status and prospects than others (Furlong et al. 2011: 363). The pathways to social reproduction are seen as more diverse and less entrenched, but the end result is again to view young people more as victims than as agents of change, rather than considering how an optimistic or hopeful outlook may be important to them (Bishop and Willis 2014).

There have been some critically optimistic forays into explaining and creating educational change, which are promising in their focus on how education involves or can enhance young people's agency. These include focusing on how children might use social and aesthetic success to overcome structural limitations to academic achievement (Skelton and Francis 2011). Critical and radical pedagogies also exist, which have long championed taking education out of its formal institutional context and giving people control over their own learning. In other words, we could get rid of schools (Freire 2006/1968; Illich 1971). This is one way to circumvent the reproduction of class within the education system, although without wider social change it has not yet been a serious alternative for most people. Other approaches have designed parallel education systems to overcome inequalities. For example, there have been successful initiatives by indigenous peoples in various parts of the world to provide alternative, more culturally appropriate, forms of education for their young people. These parallel institutions do not reject the notion of formal, systematised education in the way that Illich's (1971) proposals around deschooling do, but provide educational institutions which value indigenous knowledge and experience rather than it being a barrier to success as is often the case for those schooled within white dominated institutions (see for example Smith 2003). Also important is the much debated relationship between education and new media technologies. For example such technologies may widen access by allowing both formal and informal online learning; however, some sociologists warn of the need to consider how technologies are socially shaped, and do not determine how education is delivered on their own (Selwyn 2012). This indicates the need for a rethink of the place of the media in relation to social change.

Changing Media

Previous sociological work on the media tended to be usefully but not optimistically critical of the power of the media in shaping people's thoughts and actions and in reproducing unequal power relations. The Glasgow University Media Group (1995: 170–294), for example, spent the 1970s and 1980s outlining the ways in which media representation was biased in favour of the viewpoint of ruling elites. One instance was reports on strike action, which their analysis revealed to be skewed in ways that portrayed unions as disruptive and recalcitrant, while bosses were presented as hard done by victims. Thus the media was seen as serving the elite who owned it and reinforcing class inequalities. Similarly, various feminist and sociological studies highlighted the way in which media representations of women reinforced ideas that they were subordinate to men (CCCS Women's Group 1978; Goffman 1979; Hennessee and Nicholson 1972; Williamson 1978).

However, a critical approach simultaneously emerged which involved more optimism because it questioned how a focus on the content of media assumed that audiences were passive and unquestioningly consumed whatever the media provided (for example, Fiske and Hartley 1978). Alternative views to this 'hypodermic model' highlighted the active engagement of audiences and the variety of readings they might bring to media texts. There gradually emerged accounts of the possibility of viewing media via not just a male, but via oppositional forms of a female or black gaze (Gamman and Marshment 1987; hooks 1992) or of more fundamentally queering media texts to make them less (hetero) normative (Doty 1993). For example, in watching a television show like *Star Trek*, some audience members might imagine a sexual relationship between Kirk and Spock, thus reading the show in a different way to the more usual understandings of Kirk as a womanising heterosexual.

Critically optimistic accounts recognise the possibility of multiple meanings and presumption (combined production and consumption) in media content, thus allowing explanations of how media representations influence beliefs and actions, without completely determining them. Much more could be said about the role of media, and there are continuing debates about how the media might reinforce sexism, racism and classism (Dines and Humez 2011; Gill 2012; Wood and Skeggs 2011). However, it is not necessary to make claims that the mass media are now free from prejudice in order to recognise that possibilities exist for reading media 'against the grain' (Betterton 1987). Sometimes media products might contain more liberating or tolerant visions of class, sexual, gendered and racial difference (Van Zoonen 1995). One example might be the recent American television show *Glee* dealing sympathetically with teenage characters who are gay, lesbian, Asian, Jewish, homeless and transgendered. It is also important to remember that people do not view and interpret media in isolation, but in the context of social relations with others. For example, families and friends often watch television or box-sets together and talk about it too (Pertierra and Turner 2013). This is a reminder that peers or friends play an important role in reproducing and in changing social life.

Changing Peers and Friends

To talk of the part peers play in how individuals behave might make this sound like a textbook from the 1970s, but it is worth reconsidering the importance of other people our own age in maintaining the social world and in shaping social change. Peer group is a term rather vaguely used within current sociology, usually just as a shorthand for friendship relations (Wyn 2012: 94–5). However, not all peers are friends. Bullying classmates or celebrities of the same age unknown to a person in 'real' life, may be vital to their self-formation and how they live their lives. For example, through social networking platforms like MySpace, fans may be able to 'friend' a celebrity like the musician Jarvis Cocker and also interact meaningfully with his other fans (Beer 2008). Younger readers may wonder who Jarvis Cocker is; if they are not familiar with the 1990s band Pulp, which he fronted. Indeed I have not done a very good job of coming up with an example that might mean something to those under 40, but much sociological attention to peers does focus on young people.

A critically optimistic view of social change requires that we take seriously what young people and other same-age cohorts do for each other. Much current work on youth culture pessimistically highlights social capital, or more usually the lack of it, as crucial in whether young people are able to successfully make their way through the world (for example, Furlong and Cartmel 2007; Wynn 2012). I will come back to what 'successfully' might mean shortly. Social capital means connections to other people that can be used as a resource, and thus exchanged for other forms of capital such as economic wealth. So having family friends who are lawyers might help you get a job in a law firm and thus a good salary. However, as this example indicates, work on social capital often focuses on intergenerational passing on of bridging social capital. It is about what your parents, teachers and friends of your parents might provide in terms of opportunities that can bridge the distance between your current social location and other social fields. And although continuing interdependencies between people are recognised, social change is presented as something that happens to young people, which they must individually 'negotiate' (Furlong and Cartmel 2007: 1). Little attention is paid to how children and young people might be resources for each other and how they might create social change. They may provide forms of bonding social capital: that is capital in the form of resources exchanged within a group or community. When such bonding capital is recognised amongst young people's peer groups it is usually seen to reinforce deviance and 'bad' forms of behaviour. These 'deviant' forms, of which gangs might be one example, may of themselves be valuable in helping disadvantaged youths make their way through the world. However, there seems to be little investigation of life enhancing forms of friendship in young people's lives. Young people might not only support each other in economic adversity, when parents divorce, or in surviving abuse, but also help their friends get part-time jobs at their place of work, find hobbies they love and in other ways create a meaningful and fulfilling life and contribute to social change through everyday forms of resistance (see, for example, Back 2007; Billett 2014).

Young people engage in, and not just react to, social change and they do this together in often positive ways. Sociology currently contains rather narrow understandings of the way in which peers might find ways to act collectively in bringing wider social change. Social change can be brought about by small numbers of people who do things differently. There are a variety of small to large and 'mundane' to 'heroic' ways in which groups of people might temporarily or continuously connect to resist and challenge hierarchies. Take for example the Young Women's Movement (YWCA Scotland 2016) an organisation run for young women, largely by young women, which seeks to empower them (for other examples see Chapter 3). Some of the less coherent alternative visions of the world implicitly or explicitly contained in some collective resistance might not be easily squared with the usual middle class, White, Western, leftist, intellectual dreams of equality. What people learn from each other can be intolerance and violence, but learning this is not inevitably tied to lower socio-economic position or suffering other forms of disadvantage. The trick is therefore to understand how it is that sometimes, under difficult social conditions people learn from each other more enriching ways to live.

Summary: The More Things Change…

Critically optimistic sociology can help understand not just how society is reproduced but how it changes, and how these processes of maintenance and alteration are linked. This entails questions about whether reproduction describes the continuance of inequalities and whether change is allied to progress or improvement? Institutions like education and the media are key sites to observe processes of reproduction and change. In considering education it is important to start with an optimistic view of socialisation as a form of learning in which individuals actively engage. They engage partly through forms of reflexivity, applying what they learn of the world to shaping their lives in ways that do not just reproduce inequalities but can bring positive change. Some examples of positive change have been given, such as education becoming less elitist and male dominated and the widening of access to higher education. These gains merit some optimism, despite their limitations. Sociological accounts of education have therefore tried to make sense of why formal education is less effective in reproducing social inequalities than it was in the past. Certainly more diversity is possible in resisting that reproduction, thus there is more space for change. This is a circular argument, but the point is that reproduction and change are not opposites. Reproduction produces some change and change produces some reproduction. This is evident in how education has changed. To make sense of the altered place of gender and class differences, the concept of social generations may be helpful because it locates young people within those processes of change, depending on their position relative to social conditions and sets of meanings specific to their time. However, most usage of the concept of generations tends again to emphasise structural constraints over young people's agency. Other examples do exist, however, of attempts to explain and create educational change in ways that resist the reproduction of inequalities and enhance agency. Sociology of the media has also moved towards a more optimistic attention to the ability of people to actively change their world, rather than be the victims of the reproduction of inequalities. There are accounts that suggest that diverse readings of media products are possible and that those products can promote more enlightened representations of difference. By recognising the possibility of different interpretations it is possible to see how media can be changed as well as change people, without totally determining what they think and do. An optimistic view of change also requires understanding young people as often supported, rather than simply misled by friends.

Overall, the possibilities for change and the actual bringing about of social change are entwined within social relations like friendship as well as social institutions like education and the media. The structural aspects of social change weigh heavily on individuals, but individuals are not passive in their encounters with social change. In their very sociality, in the way that the individual is never entirely separate from others, but produced in on-going relation to them, people make social change – even if they struggle to make the social world as they might wish it. Of course, not everyone wishes for the same kind of social world, nor is everyone equally well placed within the social conditions of their time and thus they bring different kinds of resources to making their way through the world. Yet, what sociologists have defined as 'successful' ways of living have sometimes followed, rather than challenged, normative ideas about what constitutes a good life. If socially excluded or oppressed groups of people seem to find some contentment, this is typically seen as some kind of 'false consciousness' or institutionalised individualism. Thus, the next chapter turns to consider why it might be important for sociologists to think more about enjoyment if they are to fully understand people's lives.

ACTIVITY

Think about education. Imagine if we abolished schools and came up with a different way to teach children what they need to know. How could this be done? Who would be involved and how? Where would it be done?

Or talk to your grandparents or other older people about their friendships, how they worked, what they did together. How different were their experiences to yours?

Note

1. Mary Kingsley was an early version of what we now would call an anthro-
    pologist and was well known for her writing about her ethnographic studies
    of African peoples in Angola in the 1890s. Woolf is making the point that
    even highly intelligent and scholarly women had received little formal
    education, especially compared to their brothers.

2

ENJOYMENT

It is curious how hard it is to capture or describe the simple enjoyment that can be found in doing something that gives you pleasure. Novelists sometimes manage quite well. Take for example, D.H. Lawrence (1914: 196) describing a young woman's enjoyment of a rose garden in his story 'Shadow in the rose garden':

> Slowly she went down one path, lingering, like one who has gone back into the past. Suddenly she was touching some heavy crimson roses that were soft as velvet, touching them thoughtfully, without knowing, as a mother sometimes fondles the hand of her child. She leaned slightly forward to catch the scent. Then she wandered on in abstraction. Sometimes a flame-coloured, scentless rose would hold her arrested. She stood gazing at it as if she could not understand it. Again the same softness of intimacy came over her, as she stood before a tumbling heap of pink petals. Then she wondered over the white rose, that was greenish, like ice, in the centre. So, slowly, like a white, pathetic butterfly, she drifted down the path, coming at last to a tiny terrace full of roses. They seemed to fill the place, a sunny, gay throng. She was shy of them, they were so many and so bright. They seemed to be conversing and laughing. She felt herself in a strange crowd. It exhilarated her, carried her out of herself. She flushed with excitement. The air was pure scent.

This beautiful description captures something of the sensual experience of enjoyment, of how someone might feel when enjoying something: the exhilaration, the excitement, the being carried out of oneself. Sociologists seldom even try to convey the quality of enjoyment or pleasure. Even sociologists with an interest in emotions such as Norbert Elias and Eric Dunning (1986: 204) seem to skirt around what pleasurable feelings might actually feel like. In their book *The Quest for Excitement* they note that 'games are largely ends in themselves. Their purpose, if they have a purpose, is to give people pleasure'. They write about how players might move or flow together, and about tensions and conflicts, but little is said about how that pleasure might be experienced. What about, for instance, the sense of frisson experienced when as a football player you head the ball just right and it floats perfectly to an ideally positioned team mate? What of the thrill of a goal keeper who finds herself cradling the ball after a split second reaction has sent her the right way in response to a free kick? And what of the welling up of tears of joy when you see your beloved football, netball, cricket or other team win a tough game?

Much sociology pessimistically ignores evidence that people sometimes find enjoyment in their lives (Bennett 2011: 305); it assumes pleasure is due to false consciousness. In the *Oxford English Dictionary* (2006), pleasure is defined as 'the condition or sensation induced by the experience or anticipation of what is felt to be good or desirable; a feeling of happy satisfaction or enjoyment; delight, gratification'. As we will see, there are powerful threads in sociology, such as those spun out from the Frankfurt School (see, for example, Adorno and Horkheimer 1979/1944), which are sceptical about to what extent people can enjoy themselves or are merely fooled by commercialised forms of entertainment into thinking that they can. These explanations account for enjoyment as false consciousness. They propose that working class people in particular, misunderstand movies or pop music or other cultural products as fun, instead of seeing them as reinforcing their domination. Although important in trying to understand how mass culture might contribute to reinforcing class inequalities, this dismisses feelings of pleasure as mistaken. It is as though working class people do not know how to appreciate 'proper', supposedly more fulfilling, cultural products like paintings or classical music or foreign films with subtitles. As well as being rather elitist and arrogant, it tends to dismiss what working class people say they enjoy without trying to understand what that enjoyment is like.

As part of the critical optimism I am advocating as key to fuller sociological knowledge, it is vital to understand how people experience pleasure, even under difficult conditions. In considering the balance between structure (how society is organised) and agency (people's ability to shape their lives) in formulating an explanation it is especially important to avoid attributing agency only to the more privileged. In acknowledging the agency of the underprivileged there is the danger of romanticising poverty and oppression, but this danger does not justify ignoring the part that capabilities play in the quality of life that humans in various parts of the globe experience (Nussbaum and Sen 2004). However, some thinkers find the methodological individualism (a focus on the experiences of individuals) of Sen and Nussbaum's approach problematic, especially in its neglect of the importance of the state in ameliorating or exacerbating inequalities (Devereux 2001). Sen (1987) does not entirely ignore the state, but his ideology, despite his being influenced by Marxist thought, can sound remarkably liberal because of the focus on the capabilities of citizens, even if he uses these to judge governments. Although the attention the capabilities approach gives to people's well-being may seem important in efforts to think optimistically about pleasure, I will contend that a less individualised approach is more promising for creating a sociology for optimists.

In working towards this less individualised, more optimistic socio-logical understanding of everyday pleasures, this chapter will deal with central sociological concerns about the relationship between structure and agency and social change. Firstly, I will examine the temptations and yet limitations of some views of the failure of pleasure to really escape bureaucratised social structures that restrict individual creativity and maintain the status quo. These views contend that people cannot enjoy themselves in any sustained, authentic way within current social structures. Secondly, it will be argued that where sociologists do think that people find pleasure it is usually in moments of leisure, rather than work. And when leisure is assumed to be the place for life enhancing pleasure, there are those who argue that this neglects how the suppos-edly unfettered nature of leisure might ally it closely to deviance, some of which may involve harm to self and others. Yet this is not the only way in which pleasure might be transgressive. Thus, the third section consid-ers other forms of subversive and transgressive enjoyment and how they might contribute to social change. The point is to reveal how a critically optimistic view of pleasure might reinvigorate sociological thinking about how agency can facilitate changes in social structures.

Candyfloss Entertainment: Pleasure is Brief and Constrained

Arguably, one of the most pessimistic sociological accounts of enjoyment coheres under the name of the Frankfurt School of Critical Theory, which argues that most experiences of pleasure are an unsatisfying illu-sion. In *Dialectic of Enlightenment,* the most celebrated text emerging from the School, Adorno and Horkheimer (1979/1944) argue that the triumph of instrumental rationality first posited by Weber leaves little hope of human beings authentically enjoying themselves. People are argued to have been pacified by mistaken beliefs that all is well and progress continues, and by an all-powerful cultural machine robbing individuals of the very freedom it promises through a 'flood of detailed information and candy-floss entertainment' (Adorno and Horkheimer 1979/1944: xv). In this view, people are 'cultural dopes', blinded to their exploitation and thus unlikely to engage in revolutionary change.

Nevertheless, these writers have things to say about hopefulness, and thus optimism. Although they highlight the enlightenment's promotion of reason as 'the mere instrument of the all-inclusive economic apparatus', they argue that escaping this requires 'not the conservation of the past, but the redemption of the hopes of the past' (Adorno and Horkheimer 1979/1944: 30, xv). In other words, by being critical of ideas of progress by recognising the destructive elements it involves, it is possible to be hopeful about more constructive social alternatives. There is some optimism in these hopes for more enjoyable futures.

To the extent that critical theory does appear more pessimistic about the pleasures of their present, this can be explained by these scholars responding to changes in social and intellectual life such as two world wars, post-industrialisation, and (post)colonial violence. The Frankfurt School were mostly German Jews who had fled to escape the holocaust, and were faced with the historical horrors of Fascism and Stalinism. It has also been argued that where they remain pessimistic this was due to a failure to overcome the intellectual limits of traditional Marxism given that they did not fundamentally reconstitute its dialectical critique. Dialectics involves understanding the continual transformation of society and for Marxists this means understanding changes in how human beings work to produce what they need. For critical theorists, instead of labour being the basis for critical thought and for emancipation, production was seen as developing towards domination (Postone and Brick 1982). For others, the pessimism of the school can be seen as centred on their critique of instrumental rationality, that is they were critical of enlightenment beliefs in the importance of using reason to achieve goals efficiently (Bennett 2011: 302). This assumes that rationality becomes all important from the eighteenth century onwards and that emotional and moral justifications for doing things become devalued. However, there is room to debate the triumph of reason over emotions, and indeed a need to be critical of assumptions that they are mutually exclusive. Emotion informs our reasoning and reasoning can produce emotions (Holmes 2010). Reasoning is thus not always instrumental and can involve pleasure (Badiou 2007: 53).

Other sociologists trying to account for pleasure have shared with the Frankfurt School a similarly negative assessment of it as fleeting and fragile and constrained by structure. In *Escape Attempts*, Stanley Cohen and Laurie Taylor (1992) offer some brilliant insights into how people manage to extract some pleasure out of the mostly routine nature of everyday life. The book arose out of research they did into prisoners serving life sentences. It took them a while to be able to get the prisoners to explain to them what they found most difficult about their confinement, but eventually they realised that it was not so much the physical, but the mental and emotional privations, the loss of identity that caused the prisoners most suffering. Under these difficult conditions, prisoners had to find a way to 'escape'. Some thoughtlessly accommodated to the prison routine, some mentally distanced themselves from it, remaining cynical about the institution, and others deliberately committed themselves to the work they were given. As part of their escape attempts they might take up studying, filling their heads with their reading and thinking. Prisoners might turn to religion to maintain a sense of self and find 'free' areas. Some perhaps planned actual attempts to escape from the prison. Others built fantasy worlds in their imaginations, day-dreaming their time away. What is so brilliant about Cohen and Taylor's book is that they realised that this finding pleasure, these escape attempts, were not just something that prisoners did. We all find ways to escape from what they call 'paramount reality', from a highly bureaucratised and scripted social world that constrains our actions and dampens our ability to find spontaneity and unfettered fun. Thus, for example, someone might have tried to escape the dull drudgery of their life by abandoning 'a dark haired lithe companion for a muscleman, or have left the sugar works in order to take a job in the car factory, given up golf and squash for karate and ballroom dancing, exchanged Leicester for Sydney' (Cohen and Taylor 1992: 67). However, if someone migrates, from Leicester to Sydney for instance, all might be novel and exciting for a while, but eventually a routine establishes itself. The new job and new life fall into dull repetition and the 'queue at the supermarket in the new city looks the same as in the old' (Cohen and Taylor 1992: 67). They are constrained once again by paramount reality, out of disappointment they perhaps return to the UK, looking to enjoy the life they had left because it was dull and predictable. And they might enjoy it, for a while, until the boredom returns and some migrate again in search of a 'better' life (Holmes and Burrows 2012).

Brilliant as *Escape Attempts* is, to me it loses some of that brilliance at the point that it becomes pessimistic about the transient vulnerability of pleasure in the face of the bureaucratic organisation of society. For Cohen and Taylor (1992: 79), '[h]owever much we may switch our sexual partners, our jobs, our hobbies, our favourite holiday spots, we may still be faced with the intrusion of former scripts'. I like to imagine a version of *Escape Attempts* which argued that sometimes these escape attempts are 'successful'. However, to stop at saying that people find ways to escape paramount reality and find some pleasure would be thought by many to lack the critical edge that Cohen and Taylor achieve by pushing further, to argue that structural constraint triumphs in the end. This emphasis on structure over agency is fundamental to sociology and even poststructuralism has failed to really challenge the discipline's fundamentally structuralist orientation. This orientation is not a bad thing, but as many writers claim, it often leaves us at a bit of a loss in understanding how agency operates in relation to structure (see Archer 2003). Cohen and Taylor argue that agency does operate, but only in brief spaces. The assumption also seems to be that pleasure occurs only in these brief, spontaneous escapes from structure.

Is it sociological heresy to suggest that we might find pleasure in orderly and even repetitive or bureaucratised activities? To use an analogy, a swimmer may love swimming in the sea on holiday, frolicking in a playful fashion; but she may also enjoy the feeling of moving through the water as she swims back and forth doing laps in her local pool twice a week. Enjoyment of order and routine does not necessarily entail a misrecognition of structural constraint or a perverse pleasure in one's own domination. If habit guides our actions less than in the past (Archer 2003), then reflexivity may not just be used to distance oneself from predictability but to create some pleasurable predictability. Cohen and Taylor conflate structure and predictable, bureaucratised routine in thinking about escape attempts. However, to assume that 'true' pleasure can only be found in spontaneous 'escapes' from structure/routine, is to imply that there is some outside of social structure, untouched by bureaucratisation and free for authentic, self-directed pleasure. Such a space seems asocial and Cohen and Taylor can be read as saying that there is no way of living for any length of time, enjoyably or otherwise, outside of the social structure which determines our actions. Thus all escape attempts are doomed. Yet social structure is not the same as bureaucratic regimentation. This implies far more deliberate organisation of society than is often the case, where structure means a connected set of orderly rules, hierarchies, schedules and processes. It is possible instead to see structure more as a chaotic assemblage of sometimes conflicting routines, constraints and only partially scripted on-going interactions. In this case, agency is not something exercised and enjoyed in hard to find gaps in structure, but actively key in order for structure to operate. This means that pleasure may be found in imposing timetables, in doing the same thing over and over to become good at it and thus pleasure is not only found in leisure as an escape.

Leisure is Pleasure?

To assume that leisure is the most likely and freest place where pleasure can be enjoyed, is to assume that leisure does not involve work and routine of some kind. Leisure activities can involve various kinds of work. For example, there is the body work involved in going to the gym, playing sport, or attending a beauty salon (Black 2004; Featherstone 1991; Gimlin 2001; Miller 2006). Work done to look good is not confined to Western women, for example young Japanese men now work at being beautiful with the help of an expanding range of products and treatments that men use in, and to support, their leisure time and to produce their desired lifestyle (Miller 2006: 125-158). In the UK there is also the highly gendered body work done in preparing for a night out with friends, women applying make-up, fake tan and styling each other's hair. These young people also work at pleasure by developing elaborate routinised rituals of pre-drinking to get themselves ready for a night out and when they go out young women do considerable 'work' in maintaining their friendship groups by looking after each other. During or after the night out there is also repair work to do, reviewing the night out and trying to use this to avoid worrisome drunkenness and ensure a 'good night' (Bancroft et al. 2014). Enjoying yourself can be hard work.

More optimistically, just as leisure can involve work, work can involve pleasure – even paid work. Marx (1959/1844) thought that meaningful work was essential to being human and that the greater the control workers had over their work the less likely they were to feel alienated and to be oppressed. For him, capitalism is flawed in taking away that control and thus dehumanising workers. The sociology of work has tended to follow this lead and to lament the deskilling of the worker within capitalist labour processes (Braverman 1975). However, even Marxist sociologists such as Burawoy (1979) suggest that workers might find some pleasure in repetitive manual labour, or other forms of tedious work in which workers lack control, like call centres (Taylor and Bain 1999). Burawoy (1979), and Roy (1960) before him, have described the kinds of game playing that might allow factory workers to find some enjoyment amongst the tedium. Enjoyment can come, for example, in creating small variations to the work by changing the colours of material being cut. Or workers may use breaks and interaction with other workers to have fun. Roy (1960) describes this in the now famous instance of the routinely repeated joke of one worker stealing another's banana every day and declaring it 'banana time'. Although these forms of enjoyment might ultimately accommodate to, rather than fundamentally resist, the oppressive capitalist conditions of such forms of labour

(Burawoy 1979), to ignore them is to fail to understand how workers might attain some dignity, sense of humanity and satisfaction, even where their control over their work is limited.

To neglect the enjoyment people find in paid work can also obscure the gendered inequalities that arise in the ways in which paid and unpaid work are related. For example, Hochschild (2001) has argued that the pressures on family life for dual-earner families might make the home a more stressful site of work and conflict than the paid workplace. This is especially true given most men's continued lack of participation in household labour. Thus, in terms of places where people find enjoyment, the workplace may be crucial. It may be less demanding than the never-ending work for women at home and men may feel less criticised in the workplace. Hochschild (2001) notes that the workplace is also important for meeting with friends in and after work. Friendships at work are crucial for maintaining a sense of identity and for finding pleasure in work.

Globalised workplaces in the majority world, for example India, can also be places of pleasure because they offer some escape from certain structural constraints, at least for more privileged workers. Middle-class Indian IT workers often find themselves in lush Westernised workplaces, shut off from the city around them. It may seem they are trying to 'escape' India via adoption of Western modes of work and leisure. This does not mean workers are uncritical of Western culture, but it can allow enjoyment of pleasures, like drinking and romance, less fettered by family and by cultural traditions. However, these workers do not escape societal concern about them as part of a breakdown in traditional values. The pleasures found at work are not inevitably revolutionary in import, or they may provide apparently greater freedoms, which exchange old forms of domination for new. This does not mean that nothing is gained, and especially for women, the difficulties of navigating a respectable femininity within such work environments may be outweighed by the enjoyment of new forms of fun (Nadeem 2009).

Professional forms of work are perhaps more obviously pleasurable, given the greater agency offered in terms of flexibility, control and self-investment in work identities usually involved. Weber (1970:77-196) noted some of these things in speaking of the sense of vocation that professionals often enjoy. The usual definition of profession is of a line of work, like the law or medicine, regulated by an association that sets out strict training requirements, standards of performance and a code of conduct. Even 'the oldest profession', which does not really fit this definition, may sometimes involve enjoyment, as there are sex workers who say that they enjoy their work because it can allow them to develop more liberated forms of sexual self-expression and some are able to carry this into their private life

(Kontula 2008). Of course this depends upon the conditions under which prostitution is undertaken. Kontula's Finnish sex workers are not 'forced' into prostitution and often exit from it after a few years, compared to the more dangerous conditions under which sex workers operate in other contexts, for example India. However, those 'other' sex workers are not without agency, albeit usually discussed more in terms of their political protests than their individual enjoyment of sex (see, for example, Kotiswaran 2011). This evidence of some sex workers' experiences of their work as pleasurable provides a counter example to claims that sex work is universally alienating and destructive of the sexual pleasure of sex workers both within and beyond the commercial sexual encounter (Kontula 2008). The example of academia as a profession can perhaps more typically exemplify professionals enjoying work. As I write this paragraph, I am currently enjoying my academic work very much because I am on a writing retreat with postgraduate students. The highly supportive atmosphere of sitting in a lovely room together writing, or sharing tips and experiences, has reminded all of us of the joys of academic work. Academics have varying degrees of flexibility in and control over their work, although the latter may have been eroded by the rise of managerialism, of the idea that education is a product and by the demise of the public university (see Holmwood 2011). Yet the sense of pleasure has not been entirely destroyed. Academics doing research might often experience a sense of 'flow', or of action without effort which brings feelings of pleasure or happiness (Csikszentmihalyi 1997; cf. Game and Metcalfe 1996: 31–32). Not only might this more individualised pleasure be experienced, but academic work can continue to provide a sense of satisfaction in a variety of other ways. Despite bureaucratic constraints, many academics do find ways to enjoy their teaching and find it rewarding, and there is joy to be had in the kinds of collegial and community building activities exemplified in the writing retreat I mentioned above (Bentley et al. 2013). I would argue this enjoyment can be a crucial form of resistance to the very managerialism and commercialised rationales of which Holmwood (2001) writes so eloquently.[1] Pleasure is not always an individualised effort to escape from power, it can be key in struggles to challenge domination.

Pleasure and Transgression

Despite the work involved, leisure has unfettered aspects that might involve transgressive forms of pleasure which involve harming self or others (Rojek 1999). Smoking can take this form. Processes of medicalisation have, as Rojek notes, supposedly linked active leisure to good health, but also made medical explanations of deviance dominant. Yet most troublesome forms of deviance occur within leisure contexts because of the way in which leisure culture is closely connected to some degree of freedom from some forms of social control. This can be exciting. Deviant behaviour as well as many forms of leisure, especially sport, are often motivated by a search for excitement (Elias 1986). Nevertheless, there is a good deal of moralising within the sociology of leisure about leisure's proper parameters as excluding aggressive and sexual passions (Rojek 1999: 27). Some forms of leisure are 'invasive' in that they make the individual incapable of forming and maintaining respectful, enjoyable relationships with others and are used to mask this alienation. An example might be drug taking in non-sociable contexts. There are also mephitic or 'poisonous' forms of leisure; these are the ones involving abuse and harm of others. This might include, amongst other things, the fantasy and preparation work involved in serial killing, which it is difficult to dispassionately consider as a form of leisure (Rojek 1999: 29-31). Rojek suggests that it is important to consider such forms as ordinary, not as somehow extreme or exceptional, because to do so can highlight wider cultural tendencies to privilege our own feelings over those of others. By considering invasive and mephitic leisure as ordinary it is also possible to see that they have routinised aspects to them. In contrast, Rojek (1999: 31, 33) describes 'wild leisure' as about more 'sporadic and opportunity based' transgressions of the limits of everyday life, which only in some cases like joy-riding or trespassing become repetitive. Other examples of wild leisure are rioting, vandalism and computer hacking. Rojek (1999: 31) thinks that some 'margin of wildness is built into the modern social order', but wild leisure only occasionally turns into something that challenges authority, and because of its visibility it is hard to avoid sanctions for long. Thus, the ways in which leisure is transgressive are presented by Rojek as largely to do with forms of pleasure that are harmful to self or others, or fail to be transgressive in ways that bring wider social change.

There is much pessimism about the commodification of leisure as a source of individualising change that can reduce agency. For example, in introducing an edited collection of work on Chinese entertainment, Chan (2014) evaluates to what extent cultural performances of ethnic dances are still enjoyed as an authentic expression of identity, community and shared values and to what extent they must alter and change to pander to tourists and otherwise become commercialised in order to survive. As one instance, Chan and Yung (2014) argue that the commercialisation of pleasure that occurred in relation to Chinese entertainment in Singapore individualised leisure and led to a decline of community and tradition.

This is similar to Western tales of the commodification of pleasure as undermining 'authentic' enjoyment and isolating individuals from each other. Yet, if those 'authentic' forms of enjoyment rely on tradition and community, they may reproduce the inequalities attached to that past way of life. For example, they may contain limited and/or restrictive roles for women. The problem is that because commodification also routinises and standardises such forms of leisure it would seem to undermine opportunities for 'wild' or transgressive forms of leisure. The rather raucous and sometimes authority challenging possibilities of Chinese entertainment are lost, but without necessarily creating space for new expressions of identity and community that might be more equal and inclusive.

There are, however, subversive and transgressive forms of pleasure which rather than harmful or transient can contribute to social change in ways that foster respect for others and thus can cause movement towards more egalitarian relations. I take as an example heterosexual pleasure. Despite considerable efforts to consider the pleasures as well as dangers of heterosex, especially for women, there is little literature that succeeds in taking such pleasure seriously. Meika Loe (2004), for instance, may somewhat challenge the view of older women as sexually disinterested and passive, but because her entry point to sexual experiences is discussing Viagra, sexual dysfunction and sexual frustration tend to continually be centred in the accounts. Heteropleasure appears shyly and with difficulty. However, 'heterosexuality is not inevitably nasty, boring, and normative' and is 'open to enjoyment and social change' (Beasley et al. 2012: 11–12).

Transgressive heterosexual pleasures involve more superficial, temporary and unthinking deviation from the norm (Beasley et al. 2012: 5–6). By insisting on frequent sex with her husband, for instance, a wife might transgress normative ideas about heterosexuality as occurring between active men initiating sex and relatively passive women. As we saw with Rojek, and Cohen and Taylor, transgressive pleasures seldom last; however, I take issue with the implication that they are therefore of little import and make limited contributions to social change.

More everyday subversions, for example living at a distance from one's partner, can upset usual expectations of heterosexual cohabitation and reformulate couples' ways of finding pleasure. Although there may be the danger of infidelity and less opportunity for sex, living apart and then reuniting regularly may sometimes provide a romantic and sexually exciting context for heteropleasure. It might also cause couples to consider the advantages of not becoming overly familiar with each other and help women avoid being stuck with gendered forms of household and emotion work. While not ignoring that intimate violence against women is widespread (World Health Organization 2013), it is also important to try and understand how more caring and enriching forms of hetero-sexual relationship can operate in order to consider how social change is possible. Subversive forms of heterosexuality can help diversify con-structions of and possibilities for pleasure. This can undermine normative views of heterosexual pleasure as centred on penetrative sex. Alternative accounts of pleasure might involve other pleasures like reading in bed or cooking each other nice meals or making the most of hugs and of the excitement involved in anticipating next seeing each other (Beasley et al. 2012: 71-77). And the enjoyment of small everyday pleasures and acts of kindness, like making a cup of tea for someone, is not confined to privi-leged couples, but can be found in a range of relationships in a range of social contexts (Brownlie 2014; Gabb and Fink 2015). These are forms of pleasure that are about respect and care for others, and although this does not mean they are without conflict, they can move people towards more egalitarian relationships (see also Holmes 2004a).

I hope that these examples have illustrated that pleasure is not only about individualised forms of desire fulfilment, but is something often enjoyed in relation to and in interaction with others. This is not to idealise relations, relationships and interaction as full of happy harmony. However, to suggest that only a sense of harmony brings pleasure is questionable. The delights of respectful disputation are known to many and the plea-sures of leisure activities such as sport often come from physically and/ or mentally 'battling' against an adversary. Pleasure does not intrinsically serve either the powerful or the dispossessed, but neither does it float free from structures of domination and struggles for political recognition.

Conclusion

Sociology has not dealt well with pleasure, especially neglecting its everyday forms and mostly producing pessimistic accounts of people's ability to enjoy themselves. Yet people experience pleasure, despite the constraints under which they live. It is thus important for sociologists to better understand pleasures in order to better comprehend how structure and agency interrelate. This chapter has contended that such understand-ing is best furthered by developing critical optimism. This is necessary to counter dominant sociological ideas about pleasure as delicate and tem-porary. The orderly and routine may be sources of enjoyment and leisure is not a free space for pleasure but involves work. There is also pleasure involved in work. Even tedious, deskilled forms of work allow for some satisfaction and occasional fun. Where workers have greater control over their work, for example in the professions, it is perhaps easier to see the pleasures of work. This is not to ignore oppressive working conditions and the ways in which work is key in reinforcing class and other forms of inequality. In fact a critically optimistic view of why and how paid work may be enjoyed, can critically illuminate how its relationship to unpaid work reinforces gender inequalities. Equally, by examining the pleasures that globalised workplaces might offer workers in the developing world, it is possible to highlight inequalities around neo-colonialism, class and again around gender inequalities but also see those workplaces as offering escape from some forms of structural constraint. People are thus agents at work, and their pleasure in work may sometimes challenge entrenched forms of domination. Whilst many of the examples of pleasure given in this chapter seem not to threaten the capitalist social order, or other forms of dominance, they do show the importance of everyday enjoyment in finding ways not only to endure but to resist. Where profit motives extend increasingly into more areas of work, such as education and care, it is vital to see how people might find ways to please themselves and others. Leisure is not always free or harmless in its transgressions and the commodification of leisure globally can undermine the chances for more spontaneous forms of pleasure. However, more respectful forms of transgressive pleasure do exist and shape and shift social life and social interactions. Pleasure is not just an individualised pursuit of happiness, but enjoyment is taken with and through other people. Being critically optimistic allows an analysis of pleasure as not just reinforcing or returning to structural constraints, but as integral to how agency is exercised within the constraints of social structure, sometimes in ways that connect us positively to others and contribute to social change.

ACTIVITY

Interview someone in your class about what kinds of things they enjoy doing. When do they do these things, where and who with? How do they feel when they are doing them?

Compare your findings with those of others in the class. What are the key themes raised and what can they tell us as sociologists about leisure and pleasure?

Note

1. These claims about the pleasures of academic work were developed in conjunction with Chris Beasley and Heather Brook. One day we hope to write the long-planned article on 'The joys of research'.

3

FREEDOM

In the third season of an American television show called *The Wire*, which originally aired in 2004, a senior policeman who is about to retire stops his team from arresting people for selling illegal drugs within a limited area of Baltimore nicknamed Hamsterdam. Crime of all kinds reduces within the city and the better safety of the area means that health and social services can get to vulnerable people and that both those taking and not taking drugs can get care. This is an example of how legalising drugs can improve poor neighbourhoods and actually lessen rather than worsen many of the wider social problems related to the illegal drugs trade. The experiment with legalisation may be a fiction in this television show, but in Amsterdam in the Netherlands, and elsewhere, it has actually been tried and had these positive results (Grapendaal et al. 1996; Lyman 2014). Allowing people the freedom to sell and to use drugs, instead of punishing them for it, seems to have benefited everybody, so why is such freedom usually restricted by governments?

These kinds of questions about freedom are questions about power and politics and how they are used in social control, which is a term used to describe the ways in which people's behaviour is regulated by other people's expectations as well as by laws. Freedom can refer to the *freedom to* do things like take drugs or to criticise the government, but it can also refer to having *freedom from* violence or hunger. Different political systems engage different kinds of power in ways that can encourage or restrict these different kinds of freedom. Present debates about democratic political systems, based on the people electing their government, argue over how much involvement 'the people' actually still have. Some thinkers argue that we have entered into a post-democratic age where ruling political elites are more interested in encouraging the freedom of the market and of big business interests than in fostering the freedom and concerns of ordinary people (Crouch 2004).

Sociology has tried to understand political systems, but also to make sense of why some people sometimes do not obey laws and social norms and why some challenge systems of power. Power does not simply keep people down and there are a range of ways of resisting. The task of this chapter is to try and understand some of the different ways in which groups and individuals might seek freedom and deal with constraints to it. How and why do human beings consort together to criticise and act against forces of domination, or to make alternative worlds based on different values? Organised crime, social movements, swingers and youth culture are examples called upon to show how a critically optimistic view of deviance and resistance can reveal the workings of social structure and agency in a way that other sociological views cannot. Some of these different forms of resistance will be discussed as they have occurred recently in societies as various as China, the US, the UK, and Burma. The aim is to show that critical optimism can illuminate how collective forms of deviance and protest might bring social changes that facilitate efforts to recognise and respect others.

In this chapter, the strategic critical optimism I have been advocating is applied to the sociology of deviance and protest as forms of resistance to power. Much work on deviance is ready to see the opportunities harmful, violent and exploitative forms of organisation may find to flourish. Of course not all violent forms of organisation are deviant. The state has, in some countries, achieved a monopoly on the legitimate use of violence (Weber 1970/1948: 334). And deviance from norms can take non-violent yet resistant courses. As well as individual behaviours like drug taking, resistant deviance may include a range of collective activities from membership in religious cults to culture jamming[1] to peaceful democratic protest. This is not to ignore more violent forms of deviance like those occurring in organised crime, street riots, or belonging to gangs. By examining examples in a range of countries we might reconsider some major sociological ideas based on European examples. For example, Elias (2000/1939) argues that European societies and individual behaviour have undergone a 'civilising process' by which people's actions and emotions are subject to more control. That control was increasingly expected to come from within the person themselves, so for instance it became gradually less acceptable for a person to resort to violent aggression to solve everyday disputes. Similar arguments are made by Foucault (1979) about power becoming not a thing but a system that promotes individual internal discipline; rather than in the past when those in authority kept power by physically punishing people. These ideas may be difficult to reconcile with the high levels of violence against women in the majority world (Walby 2013), or the rise of ethnic violence and suicide bombing in the Middle East and surrounding regions (Hassan 2014). However, Elias is not saying violence has ceased but that its legitimate outlets have shifted and norms emerged expecting individual force to be controlled – even if those norms are not always followed. His focus on shifting power relations could potentially be applied to understand violence in relations between women and men, the State and citizens in weak or failed states, or between Global powers and local tribes. There is not space to fully debate whether Elias's ideas can apply beyond Europe (see Liston and Mennell 2009; Walby 2013), rather the purpose here is to note the need to contextualise understandings of power and protest.

In order to be optimistic about freedom a very situated evaluation of it is required. Thus, much of the chapter discusses specific examples in an attempt to draw out some overall points about the importance of being optimistic in thinking about how people resist domination. These are deliberately not the most obvious examples, but are chosen because they might better reveal some of sociology's blindspots than more commonly discussed forms of resistance. Many are examples which do not seem to encourage optimism, but for that reason they can more powerfully assist in showing its critical importance in thinking sociologically.

The chapter begins by examining the challenge of seeing the state and its monopoly on violence in optimistic terms, and explores connections with organised crime. Next there is attention to more seemingly individual level freedoms, using the example of seeking greater sexual freedom through partner swapping, or swinging. These require some connection to others. The part that young people and youth culture play in relation to greater freedom is then addressed to further discuss the connection between individual and collective freedom. The collective purpose of social movements is then discussed in the final section. It is argued the 'success' of such challenges to current social organisation is not easily measurable and should not be considered only in terms of achieving stated goals. It is important to consider the ways in which deviance might enact different ways of doing and being and remake social relations. Overall, the aim is to be critical of pessimistic thinking, not in order to berate voices speaking against domination for being 'kill joys' (Ahmed 2010) but in order to more clearly see how thinking and doing things differently can and does remake the social world and how this involves a struggle over what will make it 'better' and for whom?

The State as the Guardian of Freedom? Institutional Violence and Organised Crime

States, their police, security and armed services, can usually legitimately use violence, but it might be over-optimistic to think that in doing so they always defend freedom. A state is an organisation or set of institutions including the government, law, bureaucracy and military that rule over a territory. State violence is routinely seen as acceptable and not subject to punishment, whereas this is not the case for violence committed by other peoples or organisations. So when a state like the UK or Israel bombs people in Afghanistan or Gaza, criticism is often limited and there is no formal punishment. If an individual bombs runners at the Boston marathon or a non-state organisation like PKK (an organisation seeking independence for Kurds in Turkey) bombs Turkish targets, they are seen as criminals and/or terrorists and sought out to be jailed or put to death according to the law. However, states may sometimes use violence to control their own populations and maintain power, thus restricting and not just defending freedom. So a state like the UK may restrict the freedom of movement of individuals by keeping them detained for lengthy periods without charge if they suspect them of being involved in terrorism. This may seem to protect most people from fear of terrorist attack but at the cost of recognising an individual's right to freedom until proven guilty of a crime. So questions arise about whose or what type of freedom states are protecting and who benefits?

There are those who argue that states are not necessarily better than other organisations in ensuring ordinary people's freedom from fear or to live safely. Charles Tilly (1985) argues that states can be compared to organised crime. Like the mafia, they are a form of protection racket, providing law and order services in return for taxes. Sometimes organised crime might take over that job of protection. Varese (2011) has noted that when states are weak and perform such protection poorly, then organised crime is likely to flourish by competing with the state to protect people. Organised crime may challenge the state's monopoly on violence, but it is likely to be even harder for ordinary people to protest against say the mafia misusing their power than it is for them to protest against elected governments doing so. Thus sociologists are critical of organised crime, but also use it to highlight problems with the way the state operates.

Sociological approaches are also generally and rightly pessimistic about whether organised crime is a separate alternative to the state, given that they are often entangled. One example is the allegedly close relationship that has developed between the Chinese government and some of the triads. Chinese triads emerged in the seventeenth century as tightly controlled groups committed to restoring the Ming dynasty. By the mid-twentieth century these associations had fragmented into criminal socie-ties focused on making money (Wing Lo 2010). Originally money was generated through gambling, blackmail and drug dealing (Booth 1990); however, since the 1990s triads have fractured further, in some cases they have joined to run legal as well as illegal businesses (Wing Lo 2010: 852; see also Chu 2000). In doing so, Wing Lo (2010) claims that it is the social capital in the form of their valuing of personal connections and obligations that best explains the recent flourishing of triads in China and Hong Kong. In particular, the Chinese government allegedly sought to keep the triads onside to avoid them disrupting the hand-over of Hong Kong to China in 1997. One strategy was allowing photo oppor-tunities for triad leaders to be seen with government officials in order to give them credibility in entering into legitimate business deals. This is one example of the ways in which organised crime in many countries is often not simply condoned, but operated through the state and some of its office holders (Chamblis 1989). This valuing of status and connec-tion to powerful men has seen organised crime – including triads – now extend beyond individual states and become global in scope. Humans, drugs, sex and other commodities are trafficked between nations with these criminal networks and forms of capital supporting them (Galeotti 2005; Wing Lo 2010). Many states struggle to put an end to these activi-ties, partly because state machinery and employees are often part of them and powerful elites tend to benefit. Yet struggles for freedom take place not just at the large scale level of governments and large organisations but also at the level of relations between individuals.

Sexual Freedom for Individuals

Seemingly smaller, more individual level struggles for power contain attempts to act more freely and must also be considered in being criti-cally optimistic. Many of these bids for freedom blur the supposed public/private divide. As the feminist slogan of the 1970s put it: the personal is political. This means that areas of life supposedly private are not free from power relationships and we need to consider who ben-efits and who suffers from the kinds of social arrangements that cur-rently exist. Here I examine how some people might seek greater sexual freedom within 'swinging' relationships and polyamory. The challenge is to understand these alternatives not simply as 'escapes' (see Chapter 2) from reality, or the apolitical result of individualisation processes, but as having the capacity to remake relations to others and thus to reshape the social world. It will become apparent that these forms of 'personal' resistance are in fact also collective, even if they take place in the supposedly private sphere of intimate life.

In this optimistic view of more 'personalised' resistance, those who seek to challenge norms of monogamy through engaging in 'swinging' are not seen as individualised. Swinging, sometimes known as partner swapping, involves couples arranging to have group sex with others. Claims that swinging is a form of confluent love (a search for a special relationship rather than a special person), as described by Giddens (1992), ignore how within swinging 'individuals are prepared to put time and effort into prioritizing the [couple] identity' (Visser and McDonald 2007: 472). Swinging is not evidence of a focus on individualised satisfaction but requires the formation of communities of trust, the making of connections with others. In this sense it is perhaps more akin to intentional communities, or communes, which may share some ideological purpose or moral order (Rubin 2001; Vaisey 2007). Most swinging apparently takes place through organised swingers' groups (Rubin 2001: 721; Visser and McDonald 2007: 460). Also, swingers tend to engage in group sex in a recreational way so that jealousy does not undermine, and can even enhance, the closeness of the usually heterosexual couple who maintain emotional fidelity to each other (Visser and McDonald 2007; see also Bringle and Buunk 1991). Thus, the occasions when they have group sex are more temporary, if repeated transgressions, although perhaps undermining heterosexual monogamy without entirely challenging the couple dyad as the most important and on-going emotional relationship. Polyamory is more radical because it means having on-going relationships with more than one partner at once. It is more radical in its emphasis on building emotional and sometimes family ties with more than one sexual partner (Rubin 2001: 721). Polyamory challenges heteronormative coupling and associated living formations, although some argue it is not as heretically pluralistic as it could be (Klesse 2006). Statistics are hard to find, but one might speculate that it is a fairly uncommon alternative lifestyle. Like many non-normative, 'experimental' ways of living, there are questions about its impact on social life more widely.

Individual freedom to choose is always constrained by social circumstances, but 'life experiments' (Weeks et al. 2001) should not be underestimated in their contribution to altering how society is reproduced. Many may transgress, but not deliberately subvert dominant ways of living and thus seem to fail in bringing more widespread social change. Social change for the better is an important ideal, although there may be considerable disagreement about what 'better' might mean. Is a better society one allowing for more individual freedom, and does that mean freedom from harm or freedom to do as you choose as long as you do not harm others? Or does a 'better' society involve more equality? Not all forms of collective resistance aim for more egalitarian relations, for instance. One example is the 'promise keepers' in the United States, a highly conservative organisation of evangelical Christian men aiming to reinforce adherence to traditional gender roles within the family (Bartkowski 2004). Thus, it seems important to try to separate out ways of doing things differently which do strive for more egalitarian relationships, or at least to identify those which work at forging more respectful relations with others (Holmes 2004a). Many collective efforts to resist may not 'succeed' in this aim in the short term, but they can create spaces for greater diversity in relating to others which can facilitate social shifts in what is possible. Some of these possibilities are best seen in a brief account of youth resistance.

The Freedom of Youth?

The issue of what resistance and freedom mean in contemporary youth culture is important in assessing the future for positive change as youth resistance is 'commonly interpreted as a sign of a zeitgeist and of more fundamental changes in society' (Johansson and Lalander 2012: 1078). Contemporary understandings of resistance have emerged which see it as encompassing a variety of forms of activity aimed at bringing positive, and sometimes radical social change. More recently these have shifted from a rather unclear diffuseness to a more structurally grounded interest in resistance to intersecting forms of inequality around class, gender and ethnicity (Johansson and Lalander 2012). This shift enables a consideration of both the omnipresence of resistance in seemingly more individualised micro-politics, but more importantly, can help see how youth find more collective ways to seek change, rather than just focusing on their individual freedom to choose.

Young people are often accused of being only interested in their individual freedom to do what they want, but they do connect with each other to protest. For example, although the UK riots in 2011 did not appear to have been orchestrated by Twitter, as the media claimed, they did involve a coming together of groups acting against the state. For example, black, Asian and white gangs joined together against the police in some places (Lewis and Newburn 2011). The emphasis on the importance of social media in the protests tended to fetishise technology

and ignore the role of contradictions within capitalism and the alienation of youth in producing conflict and change (Bridges 2012; Fuchs
2012). Nevertheless, the existence of connections between the young
people who took to the streets should not be dismissed, however they
were mediated or realised. The riots were read, by media and government, not as genuine social protest but as opportunistic looting and
trouble-making by youngsters with bad parents (Lewis and Newburn
2011). It is interesting that these supposedly alienated and individualised youths obviously had some social groupings, if not networks, to
which they belonged and these were used to mobilise action. To dismiss
these kinds of collective activity as 'temporary allegiances' pragmatically
adopted by young people in order to survive risk society (Furlong and
Cartmel 2007: 4) is to ignore what they might do to reshape both micro
and macro social relations.

The majority of young people do not riot or take to the streets to join
other political demonstrations, but they may try and change the world in
other ways. The 'mainstream' may undertake more informal and individualised kinds of political participation (Harris et al. 2010) but most young
people are not apathetic. Many make what they regard as political decisions
as part of their everyday lives; they buy free-range eggs or try not to buy
clothes made under highly exploitative and dangerous working conditions. As Nathan Manning (2013) argues, in order to see this we need to do
more to free analysis of young people's political activity from old fashioned
definitions of politics which enshrine the public/private divide. There may
be limitations to what he calls their ethico-political practices, but such
practices should be taken as an important and reflexive part of political
repertoires in late modernity. And even apparent apathy may in fact be a
form of resistance when people deliberately disengage from mainstream
politics because they are fed up with politicians who seem to be from rich
elites, disconnected from ordinary people's lives (Manning and Holmes
2013). Thus resistance takes myriad forms and positive social change may
be achieved in a variety of ways, but it is possible that the more people
connect with others, the stronger their ability to bring change might be, as
the sociology of social movements usually suggests.

The 'Success' of Social Movements as Collective Struggles for Freedom

With social movements it is often assumed that only complete revolution
or obvious 'success' in attaining their goals counts as a shift towards freedom, but critical optimism suggests other possibilities. Social movements

are groups of people working together, usually either seeking freedom from oppression or freedom in the form of individual rights such as the right to same-sex marriage (see Chapter 6). One recent, if under-researched example of resistance with doubtful 'success' is the Movement for Peace with Justice and Dignity (MPJD), but it has achieved positive change. The movement arose after the death in 2011 of the son of Mexican man of letters, Javier Sicilia. Sicilia's son was one in a growing toll of victims of the Mexican government's declared 'war on drugs', a 'war' in which the US provided considerable official support. They did so because the demand for drugs comes from the US and because the violent crime between the different Mexican cartels is carried out with guns illegally obtained from America. However, the security forces assembled against the cartels have only seemed to contribute to an escalation of the violence over the last several years, and corruption is rife. It is a similar story to the one of Chinese triads above. The criminals and the authorities are very difficult to tell apart. And in addition, the ordinary people who have fallen victim to this war on drugs, probably in their hundreds of thousands, have been made invisible by government claims that almost all deaths have been of criminals or security personnel. Ordinary victims were made invisible, labelled as collateral damage. Sicilia thus became a leader who brought together individuals and organisations to protest the normalisation of violence, to bring an end to the militarisation of Mexico and to make visible these ordinary victims and the sufferings of their relatives (González 2012; Martínez 2012).

The forms of resistance operated by the MPJD were fairly conventional non-violent protest marches, and like other such marches against war elsewhere did not necessarily achieve their aims of ending or preventing the violence. However, they had less measurable but very important positive 'results' (for another example see Burkitt 2005). The MPJD marches, some in the form of travelling caravans of protest through the country, drew attention to the mass poverty existing in Mexico and evidenced the resulting marginalisation of large portions of the population as a key factor in fuelling drug trafficking and related crimes. The MPJD also responded to the transnational nature of the problem by not only marching in Mexico, but organising a caravan across the United States. This attracted international media attention to this globalised problem and drew attention to what was happening in Mexico, as a crisis, not as normal. Also the protests allowed the relatives to have the stories of their lost loved ones heard and to make them visible as human victims. In doing so, these people were able to find new strength and new connections to others, which were massively important in their struggles and their lives (González 2012; Martínez 2012).

As those suffering in various parts of the world commonly attest – joining with others to *try* to bring change, is a source of hope (Castells 2012) and people may try for a long time, before seeing success. This was the case with pro-democracy movement in Burma. In 2011, after over a decade of struggle, a democratically elected government took power. The new President, Thein Sein, met with the opposition leader and heroine of the pro-democracy movement, Aung San Suu Kyi. This was remarkable given that she had been detained under house arrest for over ten years, labelled an enemy of the state. There are questions about how democratic Burma is, given that the administrative and legal apparatus of government remained in the hands of those affiliated with the military, but there is greater political openness in the country than there has been for a long time (Hlaing 2012; Joseph 2012). Factors like continued military responses to on-going inter-ethnic conflict may continue to threaten the transition to democracy (Justice et al. 2015) but pro-democracy leaders in Burma themselves believe that there will be a negotiated transition of power toward the major pro-democracy party the National league for Democracy (NLD). Even if this involves accepting some continued role for the military in government, it is likely that they will become side-lined over time (Hlaing 2012; Joseph 2012). In such cases, hope is not a luxury but a necessity. It enables not just endurance, but some sense of agency. Even if collective protest does not bring the radical or swift revolution many hope for, it brings some form of change in how problems are seen and understood. It also brings relief from feelings of isolation and can create new systems of support amongst the aggrieved. The very act of protesting, even where the aims are not all achieved quickly or where conflict amongst protesters arises, can give those participating a sense of empowerment (for example, González 2012; Martínez 2012).

Critical optimism also means understanding the joy of collective protest. To question pessimism is not the same as saying that social movement actors' criticisms of domination make them 'kill joys' (Ahmed 2010). Ahmed is pessimistic about the pursuit of happiness because she argues it is a form of social control. She does see marginalised groups as offering alternative visions of happiness, but her portrait of resistance to dominance remains rather serious. Clearly the experience of oppression is a serious matter and overcoming it is not likely to be achieved by telling people to cheer up. However, hope of change and enjoyment of the struggle against domination are absolutely crucial and are somewhat neglected by Ahmed in her account of the pitfalls of socially encouraging certain kinds of happiness. The joy of social movement activity is not about idealised solidarity, but about the humanity and occasional fun of trying to open out to other people and ideas and work together to pro-test and promote possibilities. Hope is important because some forms of peaceful protest may face a long wait in seeing the changes they wish for start to occur, as in Burma, and because political activism can be emo-tionally exhausting. Thus, there need to be ways that social movement actors can find support and succour (King 2006). Moments of joy may also be crucial in sustaining activism, and joyful forms of protest might also be used strategically. This was the case with protests at the end of repressive communist regimes in Eastern Europe, when those protesting dealt with fear of provoking violent responses from the state by mak-ing their protests into ambivalent carnivalesque events in which joy was a crucial element. It was almost impossible for state forces to violently put down a march that was disguised as a fun-filled pet walk – including people marching with guinea pigs and goldfish (Flam 2004). Joy and fun are also crucial emotions in culture jamming protests against the power of capitalism. This involves changing cultural messages to make a politi-cal point, for example, altering advertisements to reveal the workings of capitalist exploitation. Thus a Coca-Cola billboard saying 'Enjoy' might have the word 'profit' added after it in spray paint. The creative and playful aspects of culture jamming make it enjoyable for those involved and this is crucial in maintaining this as a form of resistance and also in arguably providing a more effective foil to the glamour of many media representations of capitalist pleasure than more serious traditional forms of protest (Wettergren 2009). Joy and happiness can be key to resisting power through a variety of forms of collective protest.

Summarising Freedom

It is important to take a sociologically optimistic stance on freedom and resistance in order to understand how positive social change can and does occur. The state, and its supposed monopoly on violence, are not always used to defend freedom, but people resist attempts to control them. Sometimes other forces such as organised crime compete or col-lude with the state in offering to free people from fear, without actually making them free to live in safety. The freedom of privileged and power-ful groups is more likely to be enhanced at the expense of ordinary and vulnerable groups.

In the seeking of greater freedom for greater numbers, small everyday ways of individuals doing things differently are important. Even some of the apparently most individualised examples, like the swinger's search for sexual satisfaction beyond monogamous relationships, tend to rely on forming groups and can upset the dominance of fairly conservative and not always very liberated ways of relating to others. A whole range of life practices can contribute to freedom of choice and freedom from restrictive forms of power, whether they transgress, subvert or (less often) heretically overthrow normative, repressive and oppressive ideas and practices. However, this does not mean that people are, or should be, free to do whatever they choose.

In judging whether struggles for freedom are likely to bring wider change, knowledge of youth resistance is crucial given it may herald the shape of things to come. Youth resistance is also not as obviously individualised as often claimed, even if some versions like the UK riots are not easily compared to more traditional forms of protest. With many forms of protest it is difficult to measure just how much change and freedom they bring, especially when sociologists often study forms of resistance undertaken by a minority. More mainstream activities may appear rather more mundane, individualised or even apathetic but it is a failure of the sociological imagination if we cannot ask what seeming disengagement from previous ways of demanding greater freedom might mean?

By whatever means people struggle individually or collectively for freedom from oppression, sociologists should optimistically consider how they might bring change even if they do not achieve radical revolution or their other aims. I have given examples of movements like MPJD, which may not have ended the intransigent problems behind the high levels of violence afflicting Mexico, but which have drawn public attention to the issues and provided visibility and supportive connections for the victims and their families. Pessimism misses these important achievements that come from collective uniting in protest. The togetherness can be an important source of hope and a key form of support for what are often long-term struggles like that in Burma. The rapid overthrow of oppressive regimes is not the only path to freedom. If resisting power is more of a long, slow endurance test, then an optimistic sense of hope and at least occasional experiences of being happy or joyful are likely to be crucial in sustaining people as they seek positive social change.

In sum, critical optimism strives to understand freedom and resistance as always bound up with power and strives to appreciate when and how resistance brings forms of change that move people towards kinds of freedom entailing more respectful relations with others. If resistance and change are constant social processes then trying to be free and to free others is as important as succeeding.

ACTIVITY

Decide on a way in which your freedom is limited, for example your freedom to take drugs, to drive fast, or to get a good secure job. Discuss what things you could do to resist or challenge these constraints. Would you do these things on your own or together with other people? Would you refuse to pay speeding fines, lobby for law changes, write a blog, hold a sit in? What do you think would work best and why?

Note

1. Culture jamming refers to 'groups and individuals who practice symbolic protest against the expansion and domination of corporations and the logic of the market in public and private spaces' (Wettergren 2009: 2).

4

GOODNESS

Not everybody agrees about what it means to be good but we often rely on the 'goodness' of others. In the past guidance about what goodness entails has often been contradictory even within the same system of beliefs. For example, the Christian bible tells people both to take an eye for an eye and a tooth for a tooth and to 'turn the other cheek' in response to injury by others. However, people usually appreciate people being 'nice' to them. As Julie Brownlie (2014) found in her research, small, everyday acts of kindness are crucial to helping people cope, especially when they experience some kind of difficulty or crisis in their lives. For instance, one man interviewed for her project described how a friend came up to him after his wife died and asked if he needed any money. He didn't but he very much appreciated the 'comradeship' and care this displayed (Brownlie 2014: 135). There appears to still be some sense of morality and ethics as important in social life. That is, people still consider what it means to be good to oneself and others. Sociology has, however, often been hesitant to make pronouncements about morality (Gouldner 1970: 40; Hammersley 1999).

Thus this chapter will focus on sociologically understanding how people decide what is 'good' and 'right' and how they use this in living their lives. For much of its history, sociology left morals and ethics to the philosophers, until a resurgence of interest at the latter end of the twentieth century (Ignatow 2009; Shilling and Mellor 1998). Yet, like philosophy, sociology does deal with morality in terms of questions of what constitutes the good life. Some sociologists argue that sociology can also provide evidence for making moral decisions and show that moral betterment is meaningful and measurable (Sklair 1970). Sociology can at least help understand how people make choices and decisions about what is right and wrong and to consider how guidelines for doing so are codified into ethics. Morality is arguably increasingly important in a social world where people are not as strongly guided as before by traditional ways of doing things or by set ethical codes. Yet questions remain of whether society stops people giving in to their aggressive selfish 'nature', or hampers their inherent 'boundless altruism' (Bauman 2008: 48; see also Bauman 1995). The chapter begins by discussing how the founders of sociology dealt with morals and ethics, then critically evaluates more recent sociologies of morality. I then work towards understanding how bodies, emotions and relations with others need to be understood as part of morality and ethics. This will highlight the value of a more optimistic sociology for understanding how people identify their key concerns and try to fit them with a 'viable' (Archer 2003), enjoyable (see Chapter 2) and 'good' way of living.

What it Means to be Good is Socially Constructed

As we will see, the dominant sociological position on morals rejects the notion of universal moral truths in favour of recognising the differences of morality in 'various ages, and among various nations' (Martineau 1838: 11). Harriet Martineau has arguably as much right to be considered a founder of sociology as Marx or Weber (Hill and Hoecker-Drysdale 2001: 4), and indeed her book on *How to Observe Morals and Manners* (1838[1]) expresses what we would still expect sociologists to say. For Martineau (1838: 11), 'every man's feelings of right and wrong, instead of being born with him, grow up in him from the influences to which he is subjected'. Yet she notes some commonality in moral beliefs in that what makes people happy is thought good and what makes them miserable evil. In saying that the morals and manners of a nation should be tested in reference to 'the essentials of human happiness' (Martineau 1838: 9), she explicitly refers to emotions, which are rather neglected by the other founders, who do however mostly concur that morality is to be analysed but not judged.

Some sociologists, like Marx, appear to doubt whether morality is important at all in understanding society (Buchanan 1987: 119). His materialist perspective disputes that ideas are the driving force of history. This means he is critical of the possibility that the social world is changed by moral beliefs in freedom and reason. In disagreeing with idealists such as Hegel, Marx (1983/1932) argues that it is the human capacity for production that brings social change. This turns his attention away from conventional morality and towards the ways in which 'circumstances make men' (Marx 1983: 182). To some scholars, Marx sees all morality as drawing a veil over reality and creating a barrier to social progress. He is supposed to reject morality because he does not seem to hold with principles of equality given his denial of the right of the bourgeoisie (the wealthy property-owning class) to have their interests taken seriously (Miller 1984). Yet others argue that this takes too narrow a view of morality and that there are moral concepts in Marx's critique of capitalism and advocacy of communism and in his assessment of the justification of revolutionary action (Buchanan 1987: 119; Geras 1983: 83–4). His dismissal of conventional morality is evident in his criticism of justice and rights as preventing attention to the variety of human needs. However, in characterising revolutionary action as class war he arguably takes a fairly traditional moral view about violent means being acceptable in some contexts, for him this includes achieving the 'better' outcome of a communist society (Buchanan 1987: 119–122). Buchanan (1987: 123) goes on to criticise this position, given the empirical doubtfulness of such a 'better' society being achieved and the supposed failure to consider the importance of moral constraints. However, this philosophical criticism seems to under-emphasise what Marx could be read as saying about the social construction of morals and the difficulty of deciding on 'appropriate' moral constraints within a fundamentally exploitative social system that determines morality. In other words, we might interpret Marx as saying that it is not people's 'natural' greed that creates capitalism but capitalism that compels people to be greedy. Other readings of Marx as seeking to remove morality from his analysis (Wood 1981) are perhaps closer to what becomes preeminent in sociological approaches to morality, generally following Weber.

Weber (1970/1948: 143) suggests that sociology should analyse how people live, but not judge whether a particular way of living is good. He is held responsible for dominant sociological attitudes about moral judgements as social constructions to be rationally evaluated as they occur in others, but avoided by sociologists in making their analysis of the social world (Abend 2008: 88). According to this perspective, science, and especially sociology as a science, should not be driven by what the sociologist thinks to be 'right' or 'wrong' about the practices she observes. Rather science 'contributes to the technology of controlling life by calculating external objects as well as [human] activities' (Weber 1970/1948: 150). There have been widespread challenges to Weber's idea that value-free knowledge is possible (Abend 2008, see also Gouldner 1970). However, Weber seems to suggest that, in some spheres, especially politics, actors must formulate ethical knowledge on which to base their actions. In 'Politics as a vocation', Weber (1970/1948: 119, 121) argues that politics requires ethics because it involves 'power backed up by *violence*'. This is problematic given that: '[f]rom no ethics in the world can it be concluded when and to what extent the ethically good purpose 'justifies' the ethically dangerous means and ramifications'. For instance, he argues that political revolutions are emotional, but followed by a return to routine and in the process revolutionary crusaders are turned into more mundane collectors of spoils. They overthrow their oppressors then have to form governments and gather in taxes. In order for politicians to maintain a sense of vocation in the face of such difficulties they require both an ethic of responsibility and an ethic of ultimate ends. According to Weber, social science can observe how such ethics are developed, but not evaluate the desirability of any particular 'ultimate ends'.

Durkheim (1938: 48) is more optimistic in proposing that sociology as science deal with morality and can 'guide us in the determination of ultimate ends'. His project involves what he calls a 'science of ethics' which will understand how morality is subject to changing social demands (Durkheim 1933: 32). In his view, sociology may be primarily oriented to studying reality, but 'it does not follow that we [sociologists] do not wish to improve it'. In his view, the separation of theory from practical problems is about being in a better position to solve those practical problems. The science of ethics 'teaches us to respect moral reality, [at the same time as] it furnishes us the means to improve it' (Durkheim 1933: 33, 36).

Durkheim's treatment of morality holds up surprisingly well to twenty-first century scrutiny given the dominance in sociology of the Weberian-based beliefs that sociology should be value-free (Abend 2008: 88). This is perhaps partly because morality is not some side-show to Durkheim's model of the social world. Investigating the (emotional) social construction of moral order is arguably the driving principle behind his sociology (Abend 2008; Shilling and Mellor 1998). He endeavours to develop a science of morality capable of understanding how moral rules are emotionally produced through the social as embodied individuals collect and feel together. These collective feelings he calls collective effervescence. He sees groups of people gathered together as channelling individual passions away from satisfying individual desire and towards reproducing thought and social order. Humans are characterised as highly ambivalent about this process; they want order but want to still feel spontaneous and passionate. So getting together with others and abandoning yourself to feeling is something all cultures like to do. For example, carnivals are very popular in many cultures. This getting together and dancing ecstatically in the streets is not a threat to order and morality, as often thought, but helps people feel a sense of togetherness and solidarity which is a foundation for morals (Ehrenreich 2007).

There are 'sociologically optimistic possibilities' (Shilling and Mellor 1998: 205) in how Durkheim deals with morality, despite some seeming pessimism. He tends to the negative in his argument that modernity neglects collective effervescence and thus threatens morality (Shilling and Mellor 1998: 194–196). However, elsewhere optimism is evident, for example in his distinction between normal and pathological in *The Rules of Sociological Method* 'Normal' is defined not in terms of what is considered right or good, but as 'social conditions that are the most generally distributed'. The famous example given is of crime, which is 'an integral part of all healthy societies'. In other words, crime is not simply 'bad', it helps societies function well by setting boundaries around behaviour, it establishes what is 'wrong' and yet also shows that there is some flexibility to do things differently and thus change is possible (Durkheim 1938: 55, 67, 71). Durkheim does not believe that sociology should be value-free and he does believe in moral truth. Yet for Durkheim, the sociologist's task is to understand how morality varies and develops historically, as largely determined by social structures (Abend 2008: 89, 99). Some sociologists have more recently taken up this task.

Is it Now Harder to be Good or Do People Think About What it Means More?

Sociological attention to morality tends to take a pessimistic view of humans as more selfish than in the past. I take Bauman (1995, 2008) as the most well-known exemplar, although others such as Robert Bellah and Amatai Etzioni are noted for their pessimistic furthering of Durkheim's beliefs in moral truth (Abend 2008). For Bauman (1995, 2008), positive morality (a focus on concern for others as a good thing) is fundamentally threatened by the increasingly individualised and consumerised nature of human life within postmodernity. He argues that individual moral responsibility becomes paramount as communities are fragmented and duty to others and a degree of abnegation are replaced by the pursuit of individual and instant satisfaction through consumption. Bauman (1995: 26) is critical of postmodern forms of optimism because they hinge on belief in the free market and the ability of technology to solve problems (see also Bailey 1988: 73–6). However, the stripping away of the legislative ethics of modernity does create opportunities as well as agony, in that the 'denizens of the postmodern era are, so to speak, forced to stand face-to-face with their moral autonomy, and so also with their moral responsibility' (Bauman 1995: 43). People have little to guide them about what is right and wrong and have to make all sorts of moral decisions. For example, when the Rana Plaza collapsed in 2013 in Bangladesh, killing hundreds of garment makers, shoppers all over the world had to decide whether it was right to keep buying cheap clothes if they were being made by people working in bad conditions and unsafe buildings (Lu 2013).

The problem with Bauman's ethics is his focus on moral responsibility as individual self-sacrifice or what is sometimes called: individual bodily being for the other (Shilling and Mellor 1998). This attention to the individual's relationships with others as the root of morality is somewhat at odds with the importance he places on community and is a departure from Durkheim's much more social and emotional view of the production of moral order. It also neglects the constraining aspects of previous community based moral orders. He does acknowledge that 'integrative communities' may have problems (Bauman 2008: 24), but he does not tease out the gendered (or indeed other) constraints of community based ethics, even when affirming Hochschild's account of the spread of prevalent 'cool' emotional styles. He neglects to explain Hochschild's focus on women being expected to make more sacrifices in caring for others (Bauman 2008: 53–4). Individualisation only goes so far; someone has to change nappies, clean houses, feed others, especially the sick and the frail elderly. It continues to be women who do most of this work (see for example Baxter 2013; Sullivan 2011). Expectations of the kinds of people who 'ought' to care are moral, even ethical, in that they are codified to some degree. However, he is perhaps right that moral decision-making is less clearly and completely guided by legitimated ethical codes enshrined in religion and law and more ambivalently open to each person. Thus morality requires people to reflect on what they deem to be good and to try to act and live accordingly.

Processes of social change have not ended moral action, but require much more reflexivity in determining how to live a good life. Along with other individualisation theorists like Giddens (for example 1992) Bauman might be right about processes of detraditionalisation compelling more reflexivity in place of habit (Archer 2010), but these theories fail to be *critically* optimistic about detraditionalisation, seeing it as entangled with highly problematic individualising tendencies and thus with selfishness. Bauman (2008: 25) has proposed that a new way of thinking is required to articulate with the new hardships that human beings face. This requires 'consideration of the ways in which the current human condition could be improved and rendered more inviting to a "good" (or "better") life' as well as designating the options people must face 'if they contemplate the achievement of such conditions and such a life' (Bauman 2008: 25). However, this neglects the continued importance of ties to others in people's decision making and actions outwith the regulating force of traditional values (Holmes 2014). Greti Ivana (2014) gives the example of social media like Facebook, where people are not just selfishly trying to present themselves in the best light, but to make decisions about what is right to look at or say to people. They make these decisions depending on how strong a tie they have to each person.

People seek goodness and find good and viable ways to live, not in isolation, but through and in interaction with others. Margaret Archer's work on reflexivity is more helpful in developing a critical optimism about the possibility of morality as a collective enterprise. Drawing on Charles Peirce's version of the internal conversation, Archer (for example 2003, 2007) has produced a series of books in which she makes the case for reflexivity as something primarily done in reference to others. Reflexivity means reflecting on your circumstances and using those reflections to help act. The four types of reflexivity she sets out in her typology all reference others as key to the doing of reflexivity. Communicative reflexives actively discuss what they should do with those closest to them, and reference those others in making decisions about how to live their lives. This may mean sacrificing job opportunities for the sake of the family, or not pursuing further education because it would mean leaving close family and friends behind. The point is not to judge whether these outcomes are good or bad, but to recognise that the decisions are not made simply in terms of instant self-gratification. The motive is as important morally as the consequences (Sklair 1970: 142). Autonomous reflexives might appear more like the self-pleasing subjects of Bauman's account, but Archer is adamant that although their reflexivity may be worked out primarily within their own head, this is still a conversation with the self about what is right and this is guided by an 'ethic of fairness' (Archer 2003: 237). Metareflexives are more obviously following a set of ethics and make their way through the world in relation to some kind of ideology or set of guiding principles. However, these principles, be they traditional or new age religion, Vegetarianism or Environmentalism, typically codify 'good' ways of behaving to others. These types and examples also indicate that consumerism is not perhaps as central a guiding principle as Bauman believes. However, Archer's fourth category, that of fractured reflexives, might seem to confirm that to fail as a consumer is to fail to find a viable way of making your way through the world. The traumatised, homeless and otherwise damaged who fit this category, live in a kind of suspended animation, unable to form coherent life projects. They are existing but not thinking in ways that can allow them to plan for themselves, let alone consider others. These fractured reflexives seem to most resemble Bauman's vision of the postmodern subject, yet Archer believes them atypical, rarer than the other types. Of course, all these are ideal types and as such each real person is likely to use a mixture of these types of reflexivity. There may be times in our life, under certain conditions, where we become fractured reflexives. Metareflexives may lose faith in their guiding principles and become morally paralysed. Communicative reflexivity may be occasionally employed by those who are usually autonomous reflexives. What is key is that the vast majority of these reflexive practices are relational.

However, Archer (2010) does note that communicative reflexivity, the most obviously relational mode of reflexivity, is increasingly difficult to maintain. This is the mode she argues is most likely to reproduce natal background, to be used to live a life much like the one you were born into. However, by emphasising the difficulties contemporary society presents for such reproduction she claims that Bourdieu's emphasis on the role of habitus in such reproduction is no longer appropriate in twenty-first century social life. Processes of social change are such that '[n]othing social is self-sustaining' (Archer 2010: 276) and agents always contribute to transforming the social world, but as swift change rather than stasis becomes dominant, a reflexive imperative emerges requiring them to deliberate much more about their actions. She highlights the attention of Marx, Weber and Durkheim to the massive discontinuity in context experienced by 'the prime movers' of modernity, 'even if the very slowness of modernity allowed some contextual continuity and routinization to be reestablished for others, for example, in urban working-class communities' (Archer 2010: 283). For Archer (2010: 284–5), individualised 'personal concerns' may increasingly guide agents, but they may use their personal powers individually or collectively. In fact, she argues 'that extended reliance upon reflexivity to make and monitor agential commitments and a correspondingly selective relationality (the two being mutually reinforcing) generates an agency of reflexive, evaluative engagement'. In other words, people have to be more reflexive in deciding what is important to them, this makes them selective about who they maintain close relationships with but in a way that means they have to constantly engage with and evaluate the world. Vanessa May (2008) deals with this difficulty in her study of mothers and how they constantly have to reflect on and try to act in line with public ideas about good motherhood. The problem is that these ideas clash with other norms about the importance of caring for the self.

Reflexive engagement with the world means an engagement with others, especially if we think about reflexivity as emotional (see Holmes

2010). Thus, our internal subjectivity continues to be shaped by the social order (Archer 2010: 286) and by others, and our moral deliberations are not simply guided by self-interest. Yet Archer's model of reflexivity emphasises deliberations, and this does not adequately deal with the emotional aspects of reflexivity, with how we feel about ourselves and others and how this guides our thoughts and actions (Holmes 2010).

We Feel our Way Ethically, With Other People

If we inject some optimism we can see that most morality is felt, thought about and enacted in relation to other people. Another way of putting this is to say that reflexivity around what is good and how to be good is tied in with how we feel and think about and interact with fellow human beings. This brings to mind Carol Gilligan's (1982) classic argument about moral reasoning. Gilligan explains how cognitive development becomes increasingly complex as human individuals grow and need to apprehend more intricate biographical experiences. Whilst this is a psychological statement about individual development, Elias (2000) has made similar arguments about social processes developing complexity as society becomes more complicated. Yet both psychological and sociological theories have, until recently, neglected the differential effects of gender inequality on how reflexivity, including its moral forms, might operate. Gilligan (1977: 484) was one of the first to argue that 'the very traits that have traditionally defined the "goodness" of women, their care for and sensitivity to the needs of others, are those that mark them as deficient in moral development'. She is here taking issue with Lawrence Kohlberg's account of the six stages of moral development, the most advanced supposedly being the exercise of abstract notions of justice. According to these measures, women were typically 'stuck' at stage three in this model, tending to operate particularistic forms of moral reasoning in which not rights to act, but responsibility to not hurt concrete others are crucial. She proposes a different model of moral reasoning, which takes account of 'the effects of the diffidence prevalent among women, their reluctance to speak publically in their own voice given the constraints imposed on them by the politics of differential power between the sexes' (Gilligan 1977: 490). In other words, women can struggle to assert themselves and their sense of what is right and that sense is very much a product of the social emphasis put on their caring duties and the way in which it encourages women to consider the concrete particularities of human beings and the situations in which they find themselves connected to each other. In fact, Gilligan (1982: 100) suggests that models of moral reasoning be revised, and that recognising the particular substance of individual human difficulties may make it more possible to 'consider the social injustices that their moral problems may reflect'. For example, we might reconsider how bad it is to steal a loaf of bread if a particular person does it to feed her or his starving family. Useful as this is there are limitations to her account of morality.

Optimistically, it is possible to see attention to the concrete particularities of other people as key to moral reflexivity for everyone. To the extent that we are immersed in intimate relationships, we are all concrete others and can take account of wider social circumstances in judging what is good (Benhabib 1987: 92). Kohlberg indeed responded to Gilligan's critique partly by adding a care and responsibility orientation to his model, which he argued related to the private setting of relationships with significant others rather than being gender specific. However, Benhabib (1987) sees this as involving a problematic distinction between 'public' justice and the supposedly private pursuit of the good life. She explains how this distinction rests upon a history of sequestering women into the 'private' sphere and associating them with nature. Such sequestering allows for men, by contrast, to be portrayed as autonomous individuals, creating the illusion that they are disconnected and disembodied and learn to treat the claims of others in terms of moral impartiality. This model ignores human dependence and the experiences of women in caring for others. To take the standpoint of the generalised other, Benhabib argues, is to view others as entitled to the same rights and duties you wish to have yourself, whereas taking the standpoint of the concrete other requires seeing others as having a particular history, identity and emotional make-up. So, we might imagine a particular homeless woman who begs and spends the money on drinking as doing so to try and dull her senses to her difficult situation, which might have come about because she left a violent partner. We might reflect on what we would do in her situation and whether it is right to judge her for drinking when we might be on our way home to enjoy a glass of wine in comfort. It requires not simply asserting my rights against your needs, but the moral exercise of responsibility and bonding and sharing. It entails feelings of love, care, sympathy and solidarity.

Universalistic moral theory neglects such 'interactional' morality (Benhabib 1987: 87–91). However, Benhabib then draws on Habermas's communicative ethics as the way to develop moral guidelines, which means through discussion with others. Iris Young (1991) has ably questioned the limitations of such practices for developing meaningful moral guidelines in the context of social groups or societies characterised by diversity. Different cultures might, for example, have different ideas about turn-taking in discussions and who gets to speak about what, and these may make it hard for groups with diverse members to discuss and decide on moral guidelines for other practices. Nevertheless, Benhabib (1987) importantly highlights the need to combine an ethic of care (what contributes to well-being) with an ethic of justice (what is 'right') in order to consider rights whilst also recognising the particular needs of our fellow humans. If rejecting communicative ethics as a way forward, other possibilities must be considered for collective reflexivity about morals.

The concept of 'social flesh' (Beasley and Bacchi 2012), which describes embodied interdependence, offers a more critically optimistic way of considering the collective elaboration of moral good. Rather than Bauman's account of an individualised being for the other, or a Habermasian communicative ethic, 'social flesh' takes account of embodied relations to others. This concept offers something different to other challenges to individualised conceptions of the social world. Trust and care are the dominant terminologies for challenging individualism and for attending to social interconnection and community and the ethics that may support them. However, those emphasising trust and the lack of engagement entailed in its loss (Putnam 2000, for example), neglect bodies and rely heavily on reforming something that seems to be cognitive functioning. Meanwhile, feminists focusing on an ethic of care only deal with embodiment in the form of bodily maintenance, rather than say pleasure. In addition, trust and care languages do not really challenge liberal individualism because of their implicit concern with improving the morality of individual citizens, thus again focusing more on cognitive actors. The kind of morality endorsed is one in which altruism (a version perhaps of Bauman's being for the other) is privileged, without critically questioning the ways in which altruism reinforces social hierarchies. For example, the scholars of trust seem to imply that '[t]he rich are to remain as rich as ever, but learn to be nicer about it' (Beasley and Bacchi 2012: 105). Those recommending an ethic of care fail to question altruism, by considering care as something the altruistic *give* to the needy. This neglects the power relationships involved in such a hierarchical conception of care. Instead, Beasley and Bacchi consider social flesh as a way to stress our embodied co-existence and interdependence. They state:

> By drawing attention to shared embodied reliance, of people across the globe on social space, infrastructure and resources, the perspective of social flesh offers a decided challenge to neo-liberal conceptions of the autonomous self and at the same time removes the supposedly already given distinction between 'strong' and 'weak'. (2012: 107)

Thus an appreciation of social flesh could form a basis for understanding how ethics are collectively produced.

How certain things or people are judged good not only happens in embodied interactions, but is an emotional process. The contribution of 'social flesh' to understanding reflexive morality as relational can be furthered by adding in some thinking about emotions. It has already been noted that Archer's account of reflexivity lacks a robust account of its emotional dimensions. This hampers attempts to consider the advantages of understanding how people typically continue to seek to engage with others in emotional ways. Emotional reflexivity as a concept highlights the entanglement of emotion and reason in individual and collective decisions. Stumblings towards how to act and how to live well are guided by how people feel. Of course, people do not always know how they feel and may need to have both internal and external 'conversations' in order to figure it out. 'Conversations' go beyond the discursive, comprising gestures and other forms of dialogue (Burkitt 2012). Thus this emotional reflexivity is achieved in interaction with others. It is fundamentally social and relational (Burkitt 2012; Holmes 2010). Through these internal and external conversations, through embodied interactions and interdependencies, human beings compare their actions, practices and feelings with each other's and against what they think is typical for themselves. Individuals may gauge whether a particular act or life project fits with what they perceive as their moral identity – their sense of what kind of moral person they are (Stets and Carter 2012), but they may also seek to make comparisons, including moral comparisons, between the kind of life they live and others, especially those in similar situations. For example, some couples in distance relationships might be reflexive by comparing their thoughts, feelings and actions with others like and unlike them. This helps them try to shape a 'good' way to live (Holmes 2014: 117–124). By combining conceptualisations of 'social flesh' as accounting for a morality which respects human embodied interdependence and of emotional reflexivity as appreciating the emotional aspects of that interdependence, it is possible to craft an optimistic vision of morality and ethics. In such a vision, sociology does have something to say about the good life as one in which respect and mutual care for embodied others are to be achieved through an emotional reflexivity that is collective and relational. Rather than the Habermasian belief in developing a communicative ethics, this is founded on an optimistic belief in embodied and emotional forms of interaction as key to positive, sometimes conflict-filled, struggles over 'the good life'. More thought on how exactly these forms of interaction might work I leave to sociologists more capable than myself.

Good Conclusions

Different groups of humans tend to disagree about what is good, but we often rely on people's goodness to make our way through the world. The sociology of morals has predominantly focused on morality and ethical codes as social products and moral judgements as to be eschewed when pursuing sociological analysis. Martineau and Weber took this stance in their work, with Weber's pronouncements on maintaining value neutrality being the fount of most sociological positions on moral judgement. Marx was not convinced of the importance of thinking about morals in an analysis of history, although his criticism of capitalism and support for revolution to overthrow oppression can be read as a stance on what is moral. Durkheim did think that an understanding of morality was key to understanding the social world. He differed from Weber in arguing that moral rules are produced through collective effervescence, and although he thought this process was threatened by modernity, he maintained an optimistic position in asserting sociology's importance in recognising the variation of ethics over time and cultures and the importance of some sense of moral truths in determining desirable social ends.

More recent sociology of morality has been almost wholly pessimistic, with Bauman, for example, arguing that moral decline has occurred due to selfish forms of individualism and consumerism that may foster individual moral responsibility but fracture 'being for the other'. This is problematic because seeing morality in terms of an individual being for the other is asocial and also neglects the uneven moral constraints attached to previous social orders which emphasised the good of the many. Like most individualisation theories this is a pessimistic view of detraditionalisation, implying a rather rosier view of 'tradition' than feminist and other scholars of oppression see. Individualisation theorists may be right that such detraditionalisation prompts greater reflexivity, but they underemphasise the continued importance of relations to others in reflecting and acting to shape a 'good' life.

Some optimism is thus needed to better understand the collective ways in which people consider and go about trying to live in moral ways that feel good. In doing so Archer's work is useful because of its attention to the interactive component of reflexivity, showing the vital importance of others in how we deliberate and enact life projects. She does note that some relational modes of reflexivity are difficult under present social conditions, but believes that evaluative engagement with others is reinforced. Her model, however, does not sufficiently account for bodies and emotions.

In order to further a critically optimistic sociology of morality, more embodied and emotional models of relational reflexivity must be devised. This can be helped by returning to Gilligan's ideas about under-valued forms of moral reasoning focused on concrete others; forms she associated with women in their caring roles. However, all of us can be concrete others and engage forms of moral reasoning that recognise the particularities of other people and their social contexts. Such reasoning may be important in formulating ethical codes to guide human conduct in our present complex world, but the Habermasian vision of achieving this through a discursive process is limited because of the highly ration-alised and cognitive modes of communication it favours which falter in the face of social diversity. Instead a more embodied form of relational reflexivity is advocated in line with Beasley and Bacchi's notion of social flesh, which acknowledges human interdependence in providing for our bodily needs, sharing space and resources. To this is added a view of relational reflexivity as involving emotions. Feelings about self and oth-ers are crucial in guiding moral action and in deliberating, acting and emoting with others in trying to live a 'good' life.

ACTIVITY

Imagine the current world is destroyed and you and your classmates are the survivors who have to build a new society. What kinds of rules would you make about what behaviour is allowed and what will be punished? What kind of punishments would there be? How would you divide up work? Who would do what? How would children, the elderly and the sick be looked after?

Note

1. I quote from a transcription of this book, available online, but not carrying the original pagination, thus the pages numbers are as in the transcription. http://www.aughty.org/pdf/how_observe_martineau.pdf. The book may also be downloaded from the Harvard university archive https://archive.org/details/howtoobservemor02martgoog.

5

EQUALITY

Young African Americans probably do not worry too much about where they sit down when they go to a diner, deli or fast food outlet to eat their lunch. However, only 65 years ago in the Southern states they could have been arrested if they tried to sit at the lunch counters reserved for white people only. In fact thousands were arrested in 1960 when they sat in the seats reserved for whites and tried to order coffee. They did this as part of quickly spreading protests against racial segregation (Gladwell 2010). In a country that now has an African American president, it may seem almost unbelievable that black people, some still alive today, could once not choose just any seat when eating their lunch or catching a bus. These were small everyday reminders that they were legally considered second-class citizens. This particular form of discrimination has gone, even if racism has far from disappeared.

This chapter will approach the challenge of acknowledging positive changes, without ignoring continuing inequalities. The first section deals with to what extent equality has been achieved and 'the world we have won' (Weeks 2007) over the last 50 years or so. It outlines some of the improvements in the area of gender and racial/ethnic inequalities while noting the problems that remain. It also considers the intransigence of economic inequalities and the limits this imposes on being optimistic about lessening the harmful consequences of such social differences. The second section proposes a critically optimistic account of how striving for equality relates to happiness. This involves recognising evidence that more equal societies are happier for everyone, but also questioning how desirable it might be to achieve equality. Critical optimism can best be applied to the process of striving for more equal futures.

Focusing on the Equality Achieved

Gender equality

As well as the educational gains for women noted in Chapter 2, political rights have been extended to women in almost all countries since the nineteenth century, and not just in terms of suffrage (the right to vote). Democracy itself spread dramatically in the last half of the twentieth century with a seven-fold increase in the numbers of sovereign states with parliaments and the percentage of women in these parliaments rising from a world average of 3 per cent in 1945 to around 23 per cent by 2015 (see Figure 5.1). Currently, only four of over 150 democratic states have no women representatives in their parliaments (Federated States of Micronesia, Palau, Qatar and Vanuatu), although only ten nations have parliaments in which more than 40 per cent of the representatives are women and patterns of change for the better are more notable in some countries than others (Interparliamentary Union 2014; Paxton et al. 2010). Further equality has been enshrined in law due to the efforts of the second wave feminist movement across the globe. Women have better rights relating to bearing and parenting children, and preventing and resisting violence against women (Jamieson 1998; Weeks 2007).

Women also have greater equality in terms of work compared to 50 years ago. Increasing numbers of women have continued to join the paid workforce (see Figure 5.2), although the recent financial crisis did

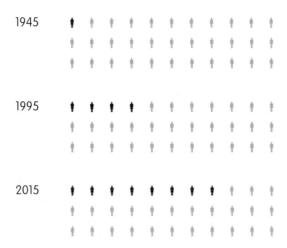

Figure 5.1 Approximate proportion of parliamentary seats in the world held by women (each ♀ represents 3 per cent)

Source: Infographic created by author using data adapted from Interparliamentary Union (2015)

lead to a drop in women's employment, in India, for example. Women are also over-represented amongst the poorest groups in many countries. For example, about 70 per cent of those in the lowest earning decile in urban West Africa are women. However, the gendered pay gap was considerably reduced worldwide by the 1990s, although there has been little shift since. An 18 per cent difference remains between men's and women's average earnings (Charles 2011; Chowdhury 2011; Nordman et al. 2011: 5137; Tijdens and Van Klaveren 2012: c). So, for instance, even in countries like the UK where the gap is comparatively low, full-time women workers earn only about 80 per cent of men's average earnings (Department for Culture, Media and Sport 2014). This is not just because women and men continue to largely do different kinds of work, because even where they do the same or very similar work to men, women earn less. Also, women's entry into professional and management positions is slow and patchy and there are limited signs of a shift in the masculine dominance of company leadership (Davidson and Burke 2011: 2–7). In Australia, Canada, the UK and USA about 30 per cent of professional and management positions are filled by women, but in China it is only 16 per cent. In Japan women make up an unimpressive 0.8 per cent of company executives (CEOs), in the UK around 10 per cent. In a recent update only 26 of the CEOs of the 500 top companies were women (Leahey et al. 2015. There have recently been slightly more appointments of women than in the past (Cook and Glass 2014: 1080) but it is not exactly remarkable progress. This disappointing level of improvement is arguably because of a 'stalled revolution'

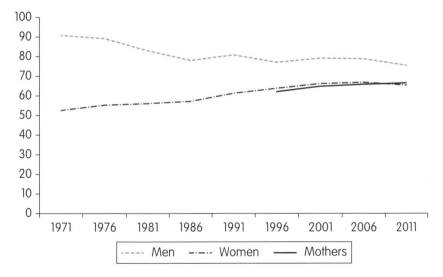

Figure 5.2   Percentages of UK adults in paid employment

Source: Graph created by author using data adapted from Spence (2011)

(Hochschild and Machung 2012: 12) in which women's opportunities at work continue to be limited by the attention to caring and home life that they are socially expected to give.

Yet entering paid work tended to have a positive effect on women's social and family status in the minority world. Men's domestic dominance as heads of household and breadwinners and women's dependence as housewives, altered in the years approaching the millennium (Giddens, 1992; Jamieson 1998; Walby, 1996; Weeks 2007). This prompted considerable concern about the decline of family life (Beck and Beck-Gernsheim 2002; 1995). However, evidence suggests that men have not substantially increased the amount of housework and childcare they do, although they may do slightly more than previously. The tiny glimmer of convergence between the amounts of domestic labour men and women do, has occurred largely because women are doing less (Sullivan 2011). Employers' lack of consideration for women's continued shouldering of most caring responsibilities, combined with the reduction of welfare provisions and the inadequate supply and quality of paid child or elder care in many countries leads to a 'work-family collision' (Pocock 2006) with which individual women struggle to cope. Many may rely on relatives or on ad hoc and shifting solutions that are creative but often fragile (Beck and Beck-Gernsheim 2002; 1995; Hochschild and Machung 2012; Pocock 2006). There may be more flexibility and independence for women in shaping their intimate and caring relationships, but the focus on individual responsibility tends to make dependency take on negative meanings and to ignore the mutual interdependence central to human living and relating (see Chapter 6). The unpaid caring work still largely done by women is crucial to reproducing society, as feminist thinking has long noted (e.g. Delphy, 1984; Hochschild, 2003). Beck and Beck-Gernsheim over-estimate the individualisation of women and their ability or willingness to extricate themselves from caring for others (Duncan et al. 2003; Holmes, 2004b; Skelton 2005). Women suffer constraints because they are more likely to be responsible for caring for others under present unequal and unsupportive social conditions. However, an optimistic view might be that dominant neoliberal discourses about personal autonomy and control are being resisted by women continuing to value such caring. Also, some women do enjoy a degree of independence, for example living alone or not cohabiting with their male or female partners, without necessarily being disconnected from others (Holmes 2004b; Jamieson and Simpson 2013).

Men's relation to women has also altered, although the problems associated with masculinity need to be understood as linked to its privileges. Connell (2011: 11-12) notes that gender equality policies include growing attention to men and masculinities. For example, men's health and boys' education programmes are paralleled to women's and girls' strategies. She points out that the problem with such attention is that it can often ignore the relational aspects of gender and heighten gender segregation. Focusing on men can also weaken women's authority in the realm of policy. There are doubts about how necessary such attention is given that men still occupy almost all of the powerful and privileged positions in governments and businesses worldwide. Yet masculinity also carries costs, with men being in more dangerous occupations, paying more tax and being the main victims of criminal assault or violence by the military; although such costs are 'the *conditions* of the advantages' (Connell 2011: 13). It is via the rewards attached to masculinity that the costs are incurred, but it is different men who are injured doing dangerous jobs to those who enjoy the comfort of the corporate executive lifestyle.

Masculinities are diverse and changing, and Connell (2011: 14-19) takes this to be grounds for optimism. There are men who support gender equality, such as those involved in action to stop men's violence against women. These campaigns occur in many different nations. Connell also cites evidence of boys exploring non-hegemonic forms of masculinity which involve respect for women. Men can and do change, especially where social and political conditions are created to encourage gender equality as in Scandinavia. Men often wish for more gender equality because of their close relationships with women they care about, be it intimate partners, daughters, mothers, other relatives or friends. They also may want to avoid the dangers to their physical and mental health that risk-seeking, doctor-avoiding forms of macho identity contain. Some men also see the benefits of more equal gender relations when their communities benefit from more flexible gendered divisions of labour or from disentangling masculinity from war. Inequalities around race and ethnicity may initially appear more intransigent.

Racial and ethnic equality?

There are ethnic divisions and conflict in many parts of the world, but there have been positive changes relating to the political and legal position of non-white and ethnic minority peoples.[1] The mid-twentieth century saw many former colonies achieve independence, and civil rights struggles in nations such as America, and Australia won political gains for their black populations (Attwood and Markus 1999; Enwezor 2001; Williams 2002). There has been improved representation of indigenous and other ethnic minorities in many national parliaments and ethnic minority politicians are elected not just to represent ethnic minority

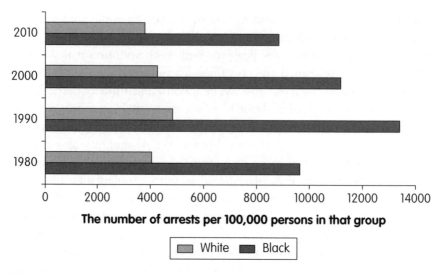

Figure 5.3   USA arrest rates by race, 1980–2010

Source: Graph created by author using data adapted from US Bureau of Justice Statistics
(2013)

constituencies. Yet under-representation is still common and can lead
to conflict (Krook and O'Brien 2010; Protsyk 2010; Sobolewska 2013).
Official forms of racial discrimination have been outlawed and new laws
introduced in many countries against inciting racial hatred or prohibiting
'hate speech' denigrating those of a different ethnic group (Bleich 2014).
Discriminatory 'Jim Crow' laws in America and the apartheid system in
South Africa may be things of the past, but informal racism has continued to be an everyday experience for many non-whites in the minority
world (Essed 1991; see for example Rollock et al. 2011). 'Institutional
racism' continues to exist, for example in the form of entrenched discrimination by the police force in England and the USA, both within
its ranks and in dealing with non-white members of the community.
As the chart in Figure 5.3 shows, for instance, black Americans are far
more likely to be arrested than whites. Yet even here shifts have occurred
(Goffman 2014; Souhami 2014), as they have in other institutions.

   The situation of minority ethnicities within the criminal justice
system tends to promote pessimism about the achievement of equality,
but optimism is crucial to solving such problems. Minority ethnicities
are vastly over-represented in the prison populations of wealthy nations
(see, for example, Alice Goffman's (2014) critical account of mass incarceration of African Americans in the USA). One of the worst countries
is Australia where Aboriginal or Torres Strait Islanders make up around
3 per cent of the overall population but over a quarter of the prison

population (Australian Bureau of Statistics 2014). In America in 2012, black males were 6 times and Hispanic males 2.5 times more likely to be imprisoned than white males (US Bureau of Justice Statistics 2013). Canada has a much lower overall rate of incarceration than the USA at around 117 prisoners per 100,000 population, nevertheless indigenous Canadians had up to 1377.6 individuals in prison per 100,000 population (Owusu-Bempah et al. 2014). Over half of New Zealand's prison population are Māori, who form around 15 per cent of the general population (Statistics New Zealand 2012). Evidence of improvement is limited, and in Australia, New Zealand and the USA the over-representation appears to have worsened (Blumstein 2015; Statistics New Zealand 2000, 2014; Weatherburn 2014: 4). However, in the US since 2010 there has been a decline in the number of First Nation peoples in Indian Country Jails who were imprisoned for committing violent offences (Minton 2014). The volume of indigenous admissions to custody in Canada may have seen some decline, but not as fast as the decline in the general Canadian population entering custody (Roberts and Melchors 2003). Despite this, some of those most committed to reducing the indigenous rate of imprisonment note that pessimism is one of the greatest barriers to change (Weatherburn 2014). Seemingly intractable problems such as disproportionate imprisonment amongst ethnic minorities require an optimism of the will (Gramsci 1978/1929: 18) if they are to be addressed. This is the case for similar issues such as poor health outcomes for ethnic minority groups in most countries, including lower life-expectancy, higher rates of heart disease, diabetes and obesity (Kumanyika 2012). Education is often seen as key to solving these problems.

Some disadvantaged ethnic groups have struggled to make gains in education, while others have experienced success. Despite global expansion in education since the late twentieth century, and national level policies and programmes to assist minorities, there has not been significant improvement in the enrolment and success of students from ethnic minority backgrounds (Hannum and Buchmann 2005; Strand 2011; Syed et al. 2011: 442). However, there is some evidence of increased numbers of ethnic minority students finishing high school and going on to college, at least in the United States (Aud et al. 2010). As the graph below shows, there is also some indication of improved achievement at high school, although the gap between black and white students in the USA has shown little change. In other national contexts, some ethnic minority groups, like British Pakistanis, pursue higher education in greater numbers and with greater success than their white peers, although that may vary according to their class and gender (Shah et al. 2010) and may alter as ethnic minority employment patterns change.

There is a rather patchy account to give of the achievement of equality between ethnic groups in the workplace. For example, the Malay minority in Singapore (around 15 per cent of the population) still tend to perform less prestigious and less economically rewarding work and are under-represented in professional and management positions, yet the smaller Indian minority are doing well (Mutalib 2012). In the USA, only 19 CEOs of Fortune 500 companies are people of colour. Since 1996, there have been 40 ethnic minority CEOs (four of whom were women) of the Fortune 500, and appointments of ethnic minority CEOs have remained fairly constant from year to year, with no increase evident. Also black managers are often promoted to weak or failing companies, thus facing a 'glass cliff'. When the company continues to decline they are often replaced by a white man (Cook and Glass 2014). Neither has the global corporate elite on the boards of the top companies in the world become more ethnically diverse, with the North Atlantic continuing to dominate, especially in the wake of the decline of Japanese companies in the first decade of the twenty-first century. However, this was measured in ways that excluded Chinese and Indian directors (Carroll 2009). The picture is likely to change as the number of Global 500 companies from Brazil, Russia, India and China (BRICs) went from 27 in 2005 to 83 in 2011 (Goldstein 2013). Meanwhile, at the lower end of the economic scale, ethnic minorities are likely to be poorer than ethnic majorities. To give just a few examples: in Vietnam, the numerous minority groups are three times more likely to be in poverty than the majority Kinh and Chinese (Imai et al. 2011). Hispanic and African Americans have poverty rates twice as high as white and non-Hispanic Americans (Gradin 2012). However, in urban West Africa, ethnic earning gaps are small, especially compared to the quite large gender gaps (Nordman et al. 2011: 5137). Employment and earning equality for ethnic minorities nevertheless seems mostly lacking.

Economic inequalities

Inequalities of income, at national and individual level, appear to have worsened in recent decades. Poor countries such as Liberia, Sierra Leone and Guinea have Gross Domestic Product (GDP) purchasing power parity of somewhere between 1,900 million US dollars and at highest estimate 12,000 million US dollars, compared to the UK's roughly 2.5 million millions and the United States' almost 17 million millions (Central Intelligence Agency 2014; World Bank 2016). Meanwhile, the wealth of the richest one per cent of the global population has increased by 60 per cent in the last 20 years (Sassen 2014: 13). In the USA, for example, this top one

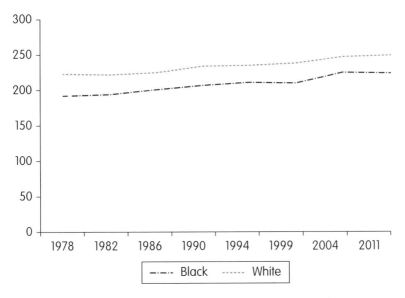

Figure 5.4 Black versus White achievement gap in average mathematics scores for US 9 year olds, 1978–2011

Source: Graph created by author using data adapted from Aud et al. (2010) and Bohrnstedt et al. (2015).

per cent receives around 14 per cent of the nation's income (Irvin 2008:17). However, much wealth lies with corporations rather than individuals, and large companies have extended their profit making. After tax, corporate profits in the United States have soared since the 1970s, and after a sharp dip following the recent financial crisis, have bounced back and risen to almost 2,000 billion dollars. However, their contributions to society in the form of tax have decreased (Sassen 2014: 19). Also in the majority world there are stark economic inequalities. For example, the Dalit caste in India, previously known as 'untouchables', continue to face discrimination which limits their access to business and ability to earn decent wages, while India's privileged classes grow richer (Thorat and Neuman 2012). Endless other examples and measures could be stated to highlight the extremely unequal distribution of wealth and the evidence suggests that across the globe the gap between rich and poor has widened (Sassen 2014).

In relative terms there are stark differences between the 'haves' and 'have nots' but there are improvements to be noted in the condition of the world's poorest people. From 1980 onwards, the 100 year long increase in the numbers of people in absolute poverty halted and a decline began. By 2001 the number of people living below the one dollar a day poverty line was 1,101 million, down from 1,219 million

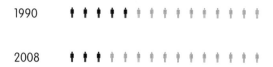

Figure 5.5   Proportion of the world's population living in extreme poverty (Each ♀ represents about 6 per cent)

Source: Infographic created by author using data adapted from World Bank (2012)

in 1990 (Kaplinsky 2005: 31–33). This meant that around one third of the world's population was living in extreme poverty in 1990 and this reduced to nearer one fifth by 2008 (see Figure 5.5). Most of the decrease is due to economic growth in East Asia and especially China, although there has also been reduction in developing countries in other regions (Kaplinsky 2005: 31–33; World Bank 2012: 2). There are some concerns about the reliability of this poverty data, as collected by the World Bank, as there are some inconsistencies. There is debate about whether the World Bank over- or under-estimates poverty, but there does seem to have been a reduction, even if not as dramatic as the World Bank figures suggest (Kaplinsky 2005: 33–34).

Why such decreases in poverty are not part of wider redistributions of wealth may require new concepts. In Europe, for example, beliefs that class is no longer a meaningful category have remained widespread amongst politicians and academics (Skeggs 2004: 5). They have even been peddled by sociologists (Beck 2007). It might be more accurate to speak of a precariat instead of a proletariat (the word Marx used for the working class). The precariat describes people who have become used to a life of unstable, insecure labour where they have no occupational or corporate identity and rely almost entirely on their money wages, lacking pensions, holiday pay, community benefits or support networks. They often have unsustainable levels of credit, rent their living accommodation, and are subject to various forms of petty humiliation. Yet they are also a growing force for change, arguing not for a redistribution of wealth but a sharing of security (Standing 2011). Meanwhile it is understandable that many may wish to disassociate themselves from a categorisation as working class which leaves them little hope for change and opens them to being judged inferior and even worthless (Skeggs 1997, 2004).

Nevertheless, the terminology of class may still be important in assessing why more economic equality has not been achieved. Some new analysis of class is already taking place, at least in the British context (Savage et al. 2013), but analyses of economic disadvantage everywhere are struggling to make sense of the complexities of marginalisation within a global economy. Within the UK and elsewhere, demonisation of those who might once have been called the working classes often appears to escape condemnation. It may even be culturally encouraged in the form of jokes about 'chavs'[2] or the negative ways in which working class people are portrayed in reality television programmes and other media (Jones 2011; Skeggs 2009). Similar cultural disparagement of 'bogans' (working class Australians, some lampooned for having money but not taste) is observable in websites like 'Things Bogans Like' (http://things-boganslike.com/). Sociology can challenge such belittling of working class people, partly by reconsidering problems around the distribution of wealth and other social goods.

Striving for Equality

One alternative to a focus on problems around the distribution of wealth is to consider how happiness is distributed. Research on the extent and degree of happiness within contemporary societies (see Greco et al. 2015) involves a central debate around the Easterlin paradox which suggests that as wealth increases, so do the expectations of individuals (Easterlin, 2001). Thus, as people get richer they become less happy (Lane 2000), or at least do not become happier. This paradox questions common assumptions that greater personal wealth will result in happier individuals.

However, happiness studies is too often interested in happiness as it relates to individual attributes rather than to sets of social relations within different times and cultures. Veenhoven (2010) provides a more sociological approach to counter Easterlin's view by looking at the social context for happiness, rather than just at individual wealth and well-being (see also Abbott et al. 2011). His analysis of data suggests that levels of happiness have become more even across class groups over the last 40 years. Whether this indicates or is the result of lessening inequalities is unclear because what might make us feel happy changes over time and varies in different countries. According to some sociologists, societies such as America have a higher propensity towards optimism – thus highlighting the positive aspects of life. Others, such as French society, tend to be more pessimistic and underline the negative aspects of life (Ostroot and Snyder, 1985). Not only how we feel about our lives, but how others judge them are important. Achieving subjective well-being relies partly on 'reflected appraisal'. Individuals appraise their life positively if other individuals judge it so (Veenhoven 2008: 47). Thus, there is no inevitable connection between wealth and happiness, but in societies where wealthy lifestyles are highly esteemed it is certainly expected that wealthy people must be happier. Yet in some very poor societies, for example Kyrgyzstan, people report high levels of satisfaction with their lives perhaps because they live amongst trusted family and friends, and although they farm at subsistence level, by doing so they maintain considerable control over their lives (Abbott et al. 2011: 217–218).

Concluding that rich people are not happy is not a reason to abandon striving for greater economic equality. It is important not to romanticise economic deprivation via the cliché of: 'they were poor but happy'. Poverty produces bad outcomes for the poor and for the society in which they survive. Poorer people have poorer health and die earlier. Societies with high rates of poverty also have high rates of violence and crime, more people in prison and lower levels of educational performance, whereas countries with more even distributions of wealth tend to have fewer of these kinds of social problems (Kumanyika 2012; Wilkinson and Pickett 2009). By switching between the individual and societal level here, or at least taking a more mid-level view of happiness in people's everyday institutional interactions (Thin 2012), we can avoid suggesting that if wealth does not guarantee individual happiness it means there is no need to worry about economic inequalities.

Being optimistic can assist in providing rationales for why striving for more equality may benefit the well-being of all. As well as evidence already mentioned, data from the World Value Survey also indicates that the more equal a society the more equally distributed happiness is amongst its citizens (Delhey and Kohler 2012). Thinking about the individual and societal benefits of more equal distributions of wealth helps provide new motivation for change (Thin 2012; Wilkinson and Pickett 2009). A major gulf between rich and poor seems to make neither likely to be happy and by working at lessening such a gulf we might better further the collective happiness of the many. Some kind of protection of those in society who are struggling is effective in reducing poverty (Fiszbein et al. 2014), but lack of welfare spending in poor countries and austerity measures which cut social welfare benefits in wealthier countries are likely to sharpen inequalities within nations.

Yet the suggestion that achieving equality will bring greater happiness for all is open to question. The question of whether equality is the 'better' future to be hoped for is implicitly behind many attempts to imagine utopia (Bauman 1976; More 1639; Wright 2010). If not, then what is the alternative? Might more equality be boring, unpleasant or totalitarian? Is achieving equality what is important or is it the striving towards it that is vital?

Critical optimism can highlight that in order to assess the importance of striving towards equality sociology requires a more complex analysis of the interrelated nature of global inequalities. While feminist theories of intersectionality (see, for example, Crenshaw 1989, Yuval-Davis 2006) offer important tools in forging critically optimistic analyses of the complexity of inequalities within a globalised world, the imagery may need adjusting. There is not space to do these theories justice, but these are useful attempts to understand the ways in which gender, race/ethnicity, class, caste, sexuality, disability and other social categories meet in the individual in ways that constrain and exclude. As Crenshaw (1989: 167) says, the goal of an intersectional approach is 'to facilitate the inclusion of marginalized groups for whom it can be said: "When they enter, we all enter"'. She is critical of seeing forms of oppression as drivers that collide to injure people, but the metaphor of intersection does suggest separate roads that join in the individual even if the joining is 'not easy to reconstruct' (Crenshaw 1989: 149). As Yuval-Davis (2006) notes, it is important to understand different types of inequalities not as added to each other but as constituting how people experience oppression. For example, a poor, black woman experiences oppression not simply as poor and black and a woman, but gender, race and class inequalities shape how she lives her life and the kind of person she can be. Although gender, race and class are forms of oppression attached to seemingly solidified, institutionalised, abstract social systems, this and other chapters have shown that they are also primarily reinforced or resisted through the imagining and doing of relations to others. Inequalities thus should be thought of not as meeting or entangled within individuals, but as like intersecting powerful illusions, overlapping in the spaces between individuals and groups and framing their real and imagined interactions. The challenge is then not only to reorganise the distribution of resources like money and food, but also to re-imagine and redo relations to others in more respectful ways.

Concluding with Equality

Critical optimism is required to carefully appreciate on-going efforts to disturb sedimented forms of social injustice and achieve greater equality. Critical optimism is only limited if we too narrowly focus on whether equality has been achieved. The evidence suggests that change for the better has been slow and partial and can go backwards. There is no inevitable force of progress, but neither is decline into harsher forms of disadvantage and division inevitable.

There is much to still be achieved, but there have been improvements; a movement towards equality. Women have, on the whole, experienced an increase in political rights, in educational opportunities and success, and

enjoy greater equality in the workplace. Progress in shifting gender inequalities at home has been slow but men and masculinities are changing
in ways that give some cause for optimism. To understand this does not
negate, and indeed may provide lessons for addressing, on-going serious
problems such as violence against women. The same is true for assessing
the rather limited improvements relating to racial and ethnic inequalities. The improved legal and political position of most ethnic minorities
is evident, although success in education is more likely to be limited to
some ethnicities, genders and classes. Disparities and discrimination in the
workplace are shifting very slowly.

Where problems remain, optimism is vital. There seems little to
be optimistic about in the continued over-representation of minorities
within the criminal justice system. However, this and other seemingly
intractable problems affecting non-white peoples will certainly not be
dealt with if they are considered inevitable, fated or simply too difficult.
Neither will worsening economic inequalities at national and global
level lose their dire, often deadly character if they are pessimistically
viewed as a result of the triumph of exploitative neo-liberal capitalism,
rather than considering that they may be part of its death knell. To aid
such considerations it is important to invoke critical optimism about the
importance of striving for equality.

Critical optimism can lend itself better to understanding how well-
being might centre not so much around money but around relation
to others. It is necessary to do this while avoiding romanticising
poverty. Despite the ubiquitous presence of conflict in human affairs,
the possibility of empathy across differences should not be forgotten
and examples can often be found behind the daily news. Optimism may
be aided by taking seriously findings which suggest that social equality
might contribute to well-being across class divides. This is not a call to
ignore the misery that can be inflicted by economic disadvantage, and
sociological analysis of inequalities needs to be reinvigorated to make
sense of a global economy which has exacerbated those inequalities
as it has complexified sets of hierarchical relations between different
social groups. Change scurries onwards and the major forms of inequality shift and interact, rather than 'intersect'. Thus the development
of an interrelational rather than an intersectional analysis is advocated
to make sense of forms of disadvantage as they occur within globalis-
ing economic and cultural forces. Gender, race, class and other forms of
oppression are not just abstract systems but fundamentally come together
in relations to other people. These relations are not like cemented,
unmoveable roads or hopelessly entangled threads, but are pliable, sometimes calcified, sometimes slippery ways of seeing and engaging with

fellow human beings. The challenge is to reshape these relations and their consequences for people's wealth and well-being, and for that optimism is indispensable. Difficult as it might be, dangerous as it might seem, to exercise a degree of optimism about the process of striving for equality, it is essential in order to sociologically imagine how to move towards more equal lives and greater human flourishing for all.

ACTIVITY

Design a video or board game, but instead of fighting enemies, buying property, or stealing cars, base it on getting education, jobs and other social rewards. What are the most prestigious things to get and what do players have to do to get them? Meet important people? Win a TV talent show? What else?

Notes

1. The conceptualisation of 'race' and ethnicity is complex, but here is briefly how I try to use these often interlinked terms. Racism is discrimination relating to the imagined category of 'race'. The idea of race is based on misconceptions (now scientifically disproven) about the connection between physical differences such as skin colour and intellectual and other capabilities and behaviours. Racial categories are usually imposed on non-white peoples to their detriment. Ethnicity is more a self-identification (although sometimes made by others) based on the shared ancestry, history and culture of groups that see themselves or are seen as distinct (Fenton 2010). Some ethnic minorities such as Scottish people in New Zealand are not noticeably physically different from the dominant group in that country and may not be discriminated against based on their ethnic identification, whereas New Zealanders of Croatian origin may also not look different but may have experienced some discrimination due to having unfamiliar cultural practices. Other 'black' ethnic minorities in other countries, like British Pakistanis, Pacific Island New Zealanders or African Americans, to name a few, face racism based on their different appearance and cultural practices.

2. A term used to denote British people from an underclass living on council housing estates who are stereotyped as likely to dress in Burberry, live off benefits and to be teenage parents (see Jones 2011).

6

RELATIONSHIPS

In June 2015 same-sex marriage became legal in all of the United States (Roberts and Siddiqui 2015). It took a Supreme Court ruling to effect this and America was well-behind other countries, but it was a massive step in recognising the rights of gay people. It was also emblematic of rapid and substantial change in the social position of and public attitudes towards same-sex relationships, at least in the Western world. Up until the 1970s, homosexuality was listed as a mental disorder by the American Psychological Association. Sexual activity between consenting same-sex adults only became fully legal across the USA in 2003. Homosexuality stopped being illegal in England in 1967, but remained an offence in Scotland, Ireland and other countries such as New Zealand into the 1980s. In the UK between 1988 and 2003 the infamous 'Section 28' of the Local Government Act prohibited schools and other local authorities from 'promoting' homosexuality and described same-sex relationships as pretend. Homosexuality remains illegal in over 70 countries (BBC 2014), but over 20 countries now allow gay marriage, with the support of the majority of their citizens. Nevertheless, not all supporters of gay rights are enthusiastic about marriage, suggesting that it is a conservative institution and that extending it to same-sex couples weakens the potential of gay people to be a force for liberalising intimate relationships (Barker 2012, Weeks 2007). Yet, the spread of same-sex marriage is part of a story of how a much wider range of types of relationships are entered into and accepted than in the past and raises questions about the force of tradition and whether people really are becoming more selfish and individualised.

This chapter argues that critical optimism can help demonstrate that intimate relationships have changed but remain strongly central to people's lives. There has been sustained criticism of individualisation theories which make an opposite claim that such relationships have been rendered fragile (Jamieson 1998; Smart and Shipman 2004). Now there is a need to go beyond a focus on individualisation. Changes in how people live their lives do not always have negative, isolating consequences and have also brought new possibilities for creating and maintaining loving bonds with partners, families and friends. A relational view of social life is crucial to sociology and relying on and caring for others is still fundamental to human life.

Some optimism is needed to critically appreciate how families and relationships have changed largely for the better, mostly because a much wider range of ways of doing intimacy exist. Changes in intimacy have involved a range of things such as a degree of gender revolution, some transformations in intimate life, broader reproductive rights, greater acceptance of homosexuality and sexual diversity, acknowledgement of sexual violence and abuse and a general expansion of intimate citizenship (Weeks 2007). The overall result is a pluralisation of ways of intimately relating. Sometimes change has occurred as a result of collective protests or gradual shifts in demographics, attitudes and practices. Along with the increasing acceptance of same-sex relationships, the kinds of moral and social exclusion previously attached to unmarried mothers has also lessened dramatically in many countries, with a sizeable proportion (up to a quarter) of children now born outwith marriage (Holmes 2014: 19–110). Domestic violence against women persists at high levels globally (World Health Organization 2013), but other gender inequalities around housework and childcare have lessened, if slowly, in wealthy nations (Sullivan 2011). The second half of the twentieth century saw some relaxing of status boundaries between the classes and sexes and considerable informalisation of regulation around sexual and intimate life (Wouters 2007). Overall the possibilities for doing family have broadened, for example more women combine paid work and motherhood than in the past, and it is possible for women to remain independent of families; to remain child free, or to live alone (Jamieson and Simpson 2013). Families are generally smaller, and women are far less likely to be subject to the difficulties of long years bearing children, many of whom may not in the past have survived. Lower fertility and better maternal health are not restricted to Western countries, as the numbers of children women have is dropping worldwide. Maternal and infant mortality and morbidity are gradually improving even in the poorest countries (Zureick-Brown et al. 2013). None of these often long-awaited and sometimes meagre changes is cause for complacency, but they should be acknowledged in our attempts to understand the long-term historical processes of change to which families are subject.

There is some liberation in the fact that people may still draw on tradition to give meaning to their actions, but it is less important than previously in providing people with a set of rules for intimate and familial practices (Gross 2005). Gay marriage is a good example of this because same-sex couples who marry might do so because they value its 'traditional' meanings of love and commitment, but they will not necessarily, any more than many heterosexual couples, decide that they should follow previous marriage practices of one partner obeying the other or staying at home and doing all the housework. Previous social arrangements around intimacy could be constricting, especially for women. These shifts away from past practices are not confined to the minority (Western) world and extend, albeit in different ways, to supposedly more 'traditional' cultures. For example, there are continuities, but 'traditional' expectations around marriage in Hong Kong have altered in response to changes such as women having fewer children and expecting to continue working after marriage (Jackson et al. 2013).

Change does not mean decline and rather than pessimistic accounts of families as becoming more fragile and individuals as increasingly selfish and isolated, I argue that a quest for intimacy remains at the core of people's lives – even under globalisation. Changes like increased geographical mobility can bring lovers together and feelings and care for others are maintained across often vast distances. Couples might meet and fall in love while one partner is travelling the world, a daughter might migrate across the globe but still tend to her parents via constant phone calls and frequent visits (Baldassar et al 2007; McLeod and Burrows 2012). One of the challenges in such relationships is maintaining intimacy without bodily co-presence. There are new possibilities but also limits to relating in disembodied ways. Social media and other new communication technologies like internet video telephony may not replace face-to-face interaction but they can help connect families, couples and friends who cannot always be together and they are used to deliver forms of care. For example, couples in distance relationships or adult children with elderly parents in another country might provide a good deal of emotional support over the telephone, or via the internet (Holmes 2014: 164; Wilding 2006).

Critical optimism encourages a view of intimate relationships as not simply about self-satisfaction but as still about caring for others, especially caring in mutual, interdependent ways. Human beings are social creatures and our very self 'arises in the process of social experience and activity' (Mead 1962: 135), thus being a product of our relation to others. We all require and rely on others for support and care of various kinds, much of it involving mutual exchanges rather than altruistic giving by the strong to the weak (Beasley and Bacchi 2012; see also Brownlie 2014). Widespread alterations in how these intimate 'exchanges' work have occurred but some of the key trends are here assessed to show the value of a critically optimistic view of the increase in people living alone and cohabiting, of the increased economic and social independence of women, and of the emergence of family and intimate formations less tied to economic survival and thus more able to be disconnected from ideologies valorising growth.

Alone But Not Lonely, Shacked Up Not Shackled?

Across the world more people are living alone then in the past, but this does not necessarily mean being single or without ties. The numbers of people living alone have increased considerably in 'developed' nations (De Vaus and Richardson 2009: 4–5; Jamieson and Simpson 2013: 34–35; Jamieson et al. 2009). From Australia to Austria, the group with the sharpest increase in solo-living is 30 to 59 year olds. Up to 15 per cent of that age group in European Union nations live by themselves (De Vaus and Richardson 2009: 8–9; Jamieson et al. 2009). Japan and Hong Kong have similar rates of people living by themselves (Ronald and Nakano 2013; Tanaka and Ng 2012). In other parts of Asia, the Middle East, and Africa, single households are less common, constituting at most 11 per cent of households by 2011 and in some places as little as 4 per cent (Jamieson and Simpson 2013: 34–35). This rise in younger people living alone is partly due to higher rates of divorce (De Vaus and Richardson 2009: 11–12; Jamieson et al. 2009), but also occurs because couples may not always want to share living space. Many of those who live alone may have partners living in another household. A recent Scottish study on solo-living indicates that about one fifth of people living alone are in a couple where their present partner lives in another household (Jamieson and Simpson 2013: 254). Wherever they are, those who live alone are still usually strongly linked to their families and continue to share in caring for others (see, for example, Holmes 2004b; Jamieson and Simpson 2013; Tanaka and Ng 2012).

The possibility of living alone, rather than having to rely on others for economic support, is relatively new. Women in particular have historically had lower wages, which made living with family or marriage a necessity. At certain times other factors like high youth unemployment and the cost or supply of suitable housing might keep adult children at home longer. Nevertheless, it is now possible for some young people to leave the family without marrying. Typically in Asia this is rare and more likely to mean having a flat by themselves as unmarried cohabitation is not considered respectable and flat-sharing is not a cultural norm. Staying at home with parents until marrying is still the typical option (Bulbeck 2009: 120; Jackson and Ho 2014: 397; Tokuhiro, 2010).

Yet for many, marriage is no longer the only pathway out of their family of origin and there has been a significant drop in people marrying over the last 30 years, as other options like cohabitation have become more acceptable. In the 1970s nearly one half of unmarried adults were marrying, but by the early twenty-first century many minority world nations had seen that drop to a quarter (Popenoe, 2009: 430–431). Although same-sex marriage is now possible in some places, the numbers doing so are unlikely to really alter these trends. Where the practice of couples living together when younger is common, the age at which people first marry has risen to almost 30 (Schoen and Canudas-Romo, 2005). However, early marriage was really only common for a short time in the mid-twentieth century, after the Second World War. Those born between 1888 and 1945 were more likely to marry and marry young, so between 1950 and 1970 first-time brides and grooms averaged around 21 years old. Prior to that first marriages on average took place between partners in their mid-twenties. After the brief period of being low, marriage ages increased so that by 2000 the average was around 26 to 28 for men and 24 to 26 for women. This has continued to rise to about 30 in the West (Schoen and Canudas-Romo, 2005; Jamieson and Simpson 2013: 48–49). Later and less marriage also occurs in the majority world. Obviously, there is much diversity. Average age at first marriage in sub-Saharan Africa has remained relatively young at about 17 to 20 years old, but this is older than previously. Factors such as the HIV epidemic have delayed marriage, and other changes in marriage trends occur as polygyny is challenged by women's vital economic contribution to families (Bongaarts 2006: 16; Harwood-Lejeune 2001: 264–266; Therborn 2004). Meanwhile in Eastern and Southern Africa by the turn of the twenty-first century there was a slightly higher median age of first marriage of 20 but in some countries like Namibia that average was over 24 (Harwood-Lejeune 2001: 264–266). These variations may relate to the alternatives to marriage that are available, for example in sub-Saharan Africa, it has been fairly usual to have sex before marriage or practice extramarital sex (Harwood-Lejeune 2001: 262). Cohabitation has also arguably been popular before or instead of marriage in Latin America since the sixteenth century (Camacho 2008: 2). However, there have also been declining rates of marriage in Pacific Asia (cf. Therborn 2004) where from 1970 to 2000 nations saw a doubling, or even quadrupling, of the proportion of women aged 40–44 who were single. It is possible that almost 15 per cent of women never marry (Jones 2007: 455–456; see also Tokuhiro, 2010). Yet, as noted, cohabitation is uncommon (Jones 2007: 455–456; Therborn 2004: 203, 217), showing that how intimate ties are diversifying does vary globally.

Where the diversification of intimate life has involved the normalisation of marriage alternatives like cohabiting with a partner these may offer advantages over previous practices. The majority of adults in countries such as Australia, the UK, and the USA cohabit when young, whether in same-sex or heterosexual partnerships (Bumpass and Lu 2000: 29; Popenoe 2009: 429; Wilson 2009). The institutionalisation of cohabitation has occurred quickly; for example, since the 1980s there has been a doubling of the proportion of people cohabiting in Great Britain and Australia. Estimates suggest that there are around two million cohabiting couples in the United Kingdom (Wilson 2009). First serious relationships are now more likely to involve living together rather than marrying. This may make it easier for young people to exit relationships that are unhappy or to make sure they really get to know someone before deciding to marry. Previously it seemed that cohabiting was likely to be a less lasting relationship than if the couple married (Bumpass and Lu 2000; Popenoe, 2009), but now there is some evidence that unmarried cohabitation or living together before marriage may result in greater longevity for couples (Hewitt and De Vaus 2009). The popularity and longevity of cohabitation may be partly due to it typically being perceived as more egalitarian. It can be interpreted as a key indicator of the way diversification in intimate life has given women the potential to eschew or at least delay the constraints commonly associated with marriage (Domínguez-Folgueras 2013). The de-centring of marriage is also associated with divorce and fertility trends that have benefits.

Better Relationships, Happier Families?

Critical optimism prompts consideration of the possibility that seemingly negative relationship trends like more people divorcing might point to positive shifts in the social position of women. Compared to the past, it is supposed that relationships, especially marriage relationships, are less likely to last. Prior to the twentieth century relationships in the minority world were likely to be brought to an end by death, and only very rarely by divorce. Yet it was not uncommon to lose a spouse, perhaps at a young age, as a result of illness or difficulties in childbirth; thus step-families were quite normal (Bailey 2003). Divorce rates in Western nations gradually increased as the twenty-first century approached (OECD Family Database 2014). Yet it was costly and difficult to get a divorce until 'no fault' divorce was introduced in a range of countries in the 1970s. This triggered a spike in divorce rates as women in particular instigated proceedings to extricate themselves from unequal and unsatisfactory relationships. That they were able to do so indicated the new possibilities for women to survive independently of marriage, due to improvements in women's employment and in welfare available (Smart and Neale 1999: 26). Eventually the rise evened off and many places have shown a small decline in the divorce rate in recent years, for example, the UK experienced a fall in the divorce rate from 14 divorcing people per 1,000 of the married population in 2004 to just over 11 per 1,000 by 2008. This fall is mostly attributable to fewer people getting married. Remarriage is also less common after divorce than 15 or 20 years ago (Office of National Statistics 2009: 63, 78). In the majority world, divorce may also be becoming more likely as a result of economic or social development, but the picture is a complex one. Chinese trends indicate rising divorce rates, with 2003, for example, showing 150,000 more couples divorced than the previous year (Wei and Qi-Yu 2005: n. 1). The rates are especially high for the more recently married with a third of divorcing couples in 2008 having been married for less than five years (*China Post* 2010). These younger women may be more likely to have employment and a degree of financial independence, making divorce an option when the marriage does not go well. In poorer countries those with little money to spare may be economically dependent on each other and may also struggle to afford the legal fees for a divorce. Cultural ideas such as the importance of family honour may make divorce almost inconceivable. In other countries, globalisation may have limited rather than increased divorce. For instance, in the North East region of early modern Japan, divorce was relatively common, ending about a third of marriages and in most cases those who divorced then remarried (Kurosu 2007: 437). Elsewhere divorce has remained uncommon. India, Ireland, Mexico and Chile have the lowest divorce rates in the world, although even these countries have experienced some rise since the 1970s (OECD Family Database 2014: 5; Rao and Sekhar 2002: 542). In East Africa there has been an increase in Black Africans getting divorced (Mburugu and Adams 2005: 18). Again, this may highlight greater autonomy for women, as can the lowering of fertility that has occurred globally, but there may also be wider benefits to fertility decline.

The worldwide decline in fertility is worth investigating as a cause for optimism rather than lament, because moderately low fertility and

some population decline may in fact lead to an improvement in standards of living (Lee and Mason 2014) and women's health, but perhaps
also to a more sustainable society (Sen 2013). Across the world it is estimated that fertility will continue to fall. It was around 2.53 children per
woman in 2005–2010, in the medium level prediction it is estimated it
will be 2.24 in 2045–2050 and drop below replacement level to 1.99
in 2095–2100 (United Nations 2013). Although drops in fertility have
occurred everywhere, it is where the fertility rate has already dropped
to below the replacement level of 2.1 babies per woman that concern
about ageing populations and government budgets has become evident
(Lee and Mason 2014). Based on 2010–2015 medium variant estimates,
and despite slight recent increases, these countries include the UK,
Australia (both at 1.88 babies per woman), much of continental Europe
(around 1.58), Canada (1.66), Japan (1.41) and China (1.66) and now
the United States (1.97) and Malaysia (1.98). Central America (2.39),
Latin America and the Caribbean (2.18) have rates that have declined to
at, or just above, replacement level. In Indonesia and India rates recently
declined to be around 2.35 to 2.5 respectively. Fertility remains well
above replacement in Africa as a whole (4.67) but rates have declined
from 5 in 2000–2005 and now vary from around 2.48 in the South to
4.93 in the Eastern nations. Other African nations with higher fertility
are also seeing it reduce. For example, Niger's rates have fallen from
7.67 at the beginning of the century to around 7.58 in 2010–2015 estimates, while Zambia's declined from about 6.00 in 2000–2005 to 5.71
in 2010–2015 (United Nations 2013). As these rates continue to drop,
standards of living may improve in poorer countries, but rather than
simply measuring improvement in terms of maximised per capita consumption (Lee and Mason 2014), it is important to acknowledge that an
ever-growing, ever-expanding number of human beings might be good
for increasing profits but bad for the planet.

In linking fertility reduction to sustainability it is important to
consider what is being sustained and to include emotions and not just
rational choices in thinking about reflexivity around having children.
While it does seem that Malthus's dire warnings that only compulsion
would reduce fertility have not come to fruition, Sen (2013: 13) is right
to be concerned about the need for sustainable development to 'take
note of political and social liberties as well as the fulfilment of economic
and material needs'. Lower fertility appears to relate to the greater
empowerment of women and does show evidence of how increased
education and social freedom can produce more sustainable population levels without coercion, or in the case of China – alongside more

coercive policies (Sen 2013: 15). Yet it is difficult for such an argument not to appear to emphasise individual abilities to 'reason and assess and choose' (Sen 2013: 14), which can make it sound as if models of liberal rational choice are being invoked. A more relational and emotional view of the reflexivity surrounding fertility practices might instead emphasise its very social and collective contexts. Sen (2013: 15) does note these contexts, especially in the case of Bangladesh where he highlights the importance of 'the expansion of family-planning opportunities, greater involvement of women in economic activities (e.g. through micro-credit movements), and much public discussion on the need to change the prevailing patterns of gender disparity'. However, he does not entirely escape more individualised, cognitive views of reason as 'thinking' and 'decisional power' (Sen 2013: 17). More emotional views of reflexivity as an interactional and felt enterprise (Holmes 2010) could be used to enhance his insights on the importance of social freedoms in securing a more sustainable future. Yet this requires that some of the concerns around lower fertility are carefully examined.

An ageing population is not necessarily a reason to be concerned about lower fertility. It is often argued that as the population ages older people will suffer from lack of younger people to care for them and to pay the taxes and pension contributions that will support them. The economy is thought also likely to suffer. However, much of this concern assumes that the ageing population will be a largely dependent one, when evidence suggests that older people are not only living longer but working longer and staying healthy longer (Spijker and MacInnes 2013).

It is also interesting to note that although fertility is low, it is less restricted to particular types of relationship. One indication of this is the substantial increase in women having children outside of marriage, at least in the minority world. For example, the UK recorded only 61,000 children born outside marriage in 1976 and 87,000 in 2009 (Office of National Statistics, 2009: 63). This may signal that marriage in less essential for women wanting to have and raise children, because they may have financial independence and because there is less stigma attached to being an unwed mother (Jamieson 1998; Weeks 2007). Outside the West, the relationship between marriage and childbearing is diverse. Many Asian countries are showing some indication of more births occurring outside marriage, although the details may differ in important ways. In the majority world there are also increases, but attitudes vary. From 1995 to 2002, teenage pregnancies in the Malay community in Singapore quadrupled despite remaining stigmatised (Jones 2007: 462). In other regions such as Eastern and Southern Africa it has long been common to have children outwith marriage or within unregistered customary marriages (Harwood-Lejeune 2001: 262). Where childbearing outside of marriage becomes relatively commonplace and detached from social stigma it would appear to indicate positive shifts towards a wider variety of family formations, many of which may be equally or better equipped to raise children than past family types.

Most families are still couples with children, or couples yet to have children (OECD Family Database 2014), but as other forms become more common there is research to be done on how well children and adults fare in them and the social benefits they bring. There may be more unmarried mothers, but they are more likely to have their children within a cohabiting relationship with the father. Children of such unmarried relationships are thus likely to spend some of their time in a two-parent family, even if by 2000 nearly half of US children had experienced living in a single-parent family (Bumpass and Lu 2000). Across the OECD countries, one tenth of all households are single parent families. Meanwhile the proportion of couple families has decreased and the number of couples without children has increased (OECD Family Database 2014). Thus, around half of families in OECD countries at least are not nuclear; they do not conform to the previous normative view of *the* family as consisting of mother, father and children sharing a household. The question is whether this is simply the next step in the change from the dominance of extended families to that of nuclear families by the 1950s, and from then greater diversification in family forms (Jamieson 1998)? Rather than warrant concern as a problem I suggest that there is cause for optimism about this diversification as offering different ways of relating that may be more equal and sustainable.

Conclusion

As intimate relationships diversify, a range of trends have been identified as causes for concern. This chapter has endeavoured to evaluate some of these trends with the aid of a critical optimism. Thus, although more people are living alone, evidence suggests that most are not without social ties, they are not lonely. In fact, living alone indicates that people are able to enjoy some independence from their families while continuing to enjoy support. This may be especially significant for women, as they are able to exercise greater autonomy over their lives. This improvement in women's status is also reflected in the fact that fewer people are marrying. For women this indicates less financial dependence on men.

Declines in marriage rates do not, however, indicate that there is less intimacy, but that different ways of doing intimacy are now possible. One is cohabitation, the rise of which in part explains why more people delay or forego marriage. Unmarried cohabitation remains a largely minority world practice, but versions of it are said to have had a history and continued presence in parts of Africa and in Latin America. The lure of cohabitation may be its promise of more egalitarian relationships, especially for heterosexuals, although that is not always what will occur. The rise may simply be one indicator of the wider diversification of intimate life.

Other areas of concern about families may also indicate improved economic and social freedoms, especially for women. Higher divorce rates for example, may indicate that more women may enjoy the means to escape unsatisfying or even violent relationships. In the majority world there may be similar improvements, although sometimes (neo) colonialism has fettered people to, rather than freed them from, restrictive marriage ties. Neither is it obvious that lower fertility is inevitably disastrous. Having fewer children may be better for women's health and well-being, it can improve standards of living and perhaps aid environmental sustainability. In considering how this might be, it is important to understand reflexivity around fertility as emotional and relational, rather than as an individual choice. Further research on this is needed in order to see how lower fertility might be crucial to creating a more sustainable society that respects social and political freedoms. In relational terms, there is evidence that an ageing population connected to lower fertility will not necessarily mean a burden of care. Older people are increasingly likely to go on contributing to society longer and to stay in good health. For those who do have children, many more now do so outside of marriage. A reduction in stigma is evident and unmarried childbearing could signal women's ability to exercise more control over the conditions under which they have, or do not have children. However, gendered relationships have shifted in a patchy fashion, so that although choices around intimate relationships have expanded, gendered divisions of labour within them still typically entrench men's privilege.

Although most families are still couple families, it is clear that a much wider range of intimate practices exist than in the past and that because of this more equitable ways of relating become more possible for more people. Whether some of these ways of living might also enhance sustainability has been touched on. The next chapter will look further at sustainability as part of considering why a critical optimism about nature and the environment is vital in current sociological thinking.

ACTIVITY

Come up with and discuss alternative ways to raise children apart from within nuclear families with a mother and father. These might include other family forms but also ideas like having giant, collectively run nurseries. Debate the strengths and limitations of the different suggestions made.

7

NATURE

Almost every day there is news of extreme weather and associated natural disasters. This previous summer there were reports of wild fires rushing across parts of America. Whole neighbourhoods were razed to the ground as the voracious flames spread easily across areas dried to tinder by prolonged droughts and hot weather. In the South West of Britain there were floods following high summer rainfall. Cars were swept away and streets blocked. Too much or too little rain have long caused problems for human societies, but scientists believe that these kinds of events are happening with greater frequency and that they are linked to climate change. There is a high level of scientific consensus about the climate as undergoing dramatic alterations and about this as being caused by human activity. Human abuse of the environment is in danger of altering climactic conditions to the point that social life as we know it may be threatened. The predictions are often dire, but the need for optimism is thus arguably even greater.

The concern of this chapter is to consider the role of critical optimism in furthering understanding of human relations with nature and animals. Most sociologists contest the idea that humans are driven entirely by 'natural' or biological rather than social processes. Early sociology was often closely allied with biology but the two disciplines diverged (see Chapter 9). While recognising that it is through bodies that humans interact, the focus of sociologists is on the social production of those bodies, rather than on their biological capabilities and processes. Much mainstream biology therefore is studying humans in a different way to sociologists and the knowledge gained is highly valuable for appreciating how our bodies work. The field of sociobiology, however, tries to explain a wide range of human behaviour via reference to biology and specifically via reference to neo-Darwinian evolutionary theory (Nielsen 1994: 267). I begin the chapter with a brief criticism of some of the ideas in that field. However, in recent years sociologists have tried to rethink the boundaries of sociology (Karakayali 2014), especially boundaries with biology and other natural sciences, in order to address some of the pressing social questions of our time. In the second section I discuss relatively recent sociological efforts to better understand our relations with other animals. Finally I examine a sociological return to 'nature' as the discipline engages with human impact on the environment, especially in the form of climate change. Here in dealing with threats to future human society, the need to be critically optimistic is both necessary and surprisingly evident.

It is Not 'Natural': Sociological Challenges to Biological Determinism

Sociology can reveal the problematically pessimistic assumptions of attempts to explain human behaviour as driven only by biological, inherited or evolutionary traits. Chapter 9 will explain some of the historical reasons for sociology's departure from its originally close alliance with biology, but here I try to appreciate why sociology appears to have returned to 'nature'. To do this it is vital to examine, from a different angle, why sociologists have remained keen to demarcate their discipline from biology, or at least certain branches of it. However, the most well-known disagreement about how to explain human actions took place between evolutionary biologists themselves in the 1970s in response to the publication of E.O. Wilson's (1975) manifesto-like *Sociobiology: The New Synthesis*. It was strongly criticised by his more Marxist or leftist-oriented colleagues Stephen Jay Gould and Richard Lewontin (see, for example, Lewontin 1976; Rose et al. 1984). I draw on some of these and other criticisms to explain why sociologists might continue to be wary of certain biological explanations for human behaviour.

Sociobiology has been criticised by sociologists because it is easily co-opted to justify rather than challenge social inequalities. For example, evolutionary psychology is one version of sociobiology in which gender and sexuality are 'presented as natural facts', as part of human nature and therefore seen as fixed in ways it would be dangerous to alter (Jackson and Rees 2007: 918, 923). Not all forms of sociobiology justify hierarchies in this way (Laland and Brown 2011), for example, Nielsen (1994: 283-284) tends to use male competition for females as an explanation for hierarchies, but one which it is implied has negative consequences such as women being treated as commodities, double standards in adultery laws and 'generally men's "proprietary" view of women's sexuality and reproductive capacity'. He thus claims that 'the emerging sociobiological view is clearly compatible with a strong feminist orientation' (Nielsen 1994: 291). There are also feminist evolutionary biologists such as Sandra Hrdy (2000) with their own careful criticisms of what their discipline has had to say about gender and sexuality. For sociologists it is how these accounts are taken up and used that is important (Jackson and Rees 2007). Sociologists are particularly critical of people using such explanations to support the dominance of certain social groups. For example, ideas taken from sociobiology are used to claim that the dominance of men over women, or white people over black is 'natural' and therefore normal, 'good' and not to be changed. Sociologists challenge these claims.

Sociologists have also critically distanced themselves from those who use biological explanations of human actions in ways which ignore social complexity and can appear to deride diversity. These explanations are reductionist, they reduce the complicated messiness of people down to biological factors. Again taking evolutionary psychology as an example of sociobiological explanations, all of human social life 'is made reducible to the heterosexual, reproductive imperative' (Jackson and Rees 2007: 918). This assumes that human actions are prompted only by a desire to reproduce by having babies. Other biologists such as Richard Lewontin (1976: 23) argue that sexual selection is just one mechanism for natural selection but is given 'considerable weight' in sociobiological explanations of behaviour. This ignores the range of complex social and cultural factors impacting on how humans act and leaves many questions, for instance about how to explain same-sex relationships. A reductionist focus can also make sociobiology likely to pathologise family forms not based on a heterosexual couple who are biological parents. For instance, some sociobiologists claim that there is 'a possible relationship in modern industrial societies between the presence in the household of an adult not biologically related to the child, such as a step-parent, and the risk of death or abuse' (Nielsen 1994: 287). The first problem here is the claim that step-parents are more likely to abuse or kill their step-children than biological parents; a claim disputed by others based on large scale survey data showing no significant differences in rates or severity of violence between genetically related and non-genetically related carers of children (Gelles and Harrop 1991; Malkin and Lamb 1994). Notice that much of this controversy occurs in the 1990s when concerns about the rise of single parent and step-families were arguably at their height. In this context, there were strong political attempts to bolster 'traditional' two-parent families and any abuse by step-parents may have been more visible because it is possible they were more likely than biological parents to be under some kind of welfare based state surveillance (Smart and

Neale 1999). The second problem is the explanation sociobiologists give for the allegedly higher rate of abuse amongst step-parents: that, like other animals, the 'male thereby prevents the females from devoting resources to another male's offspring' (Nielsen 1994: 287). Never mind that there is no mention of whether this applies to step-mothers, even if we accept the dubious claim that step-fathers are more likely to abuse step-children than biological fathers are their biological children, there are a range of complex explanations possible. For example, within patriarchal societies there is often a failure to punish men who use sex to exert power over women and children, and indeed there are often rewards for men's violence against women. This applies not just to step-fathers (Brownmiller 1975; Wade et al. 2014). However, if men (and women?) are biologically driven to prefer their own offspring, how can we explain the many step, blended, adopted and other families where 'parents' devote considerable emotional and material resources to raising children to whom they are not biologically related (Hamilton et al. 2007; Smart and Neale 1999; Weeks et al. 2001)? For that, more sociologically informed investigations are needed, in this case involving some 'optimism' in the form of critical questioning of common-sense assumptions that non-biologically based parenting is deficient.

The very simplicity of sociobiology gives it wide appeal, but can raise questions about the 'scientific' basis of its claims. As noted, a key idea within sociobiology is that women and men's actions are guided by their desire to pass on their genes through sex and reproduction. Especially when such theories are filtered through the media, the nuances are frequently lost (Jackson and Rees 2007: 919–920). Yet even popularisation of these ideas written by scientists might have their flaws. One example is the popular book *The Selfish Gene* (Dawkins 1989 [1976]). By calling a gene selfish Dawkins is suggesting that genes replicate in ways that increase their own chances of survival at the expense of others, including the human or animal of which they are part (Dawkins 1989[1976]: 4). This is not meant to imply that genes have a will of their own, but that evolutionary processes can be talked about in this way to show how they operate at the level of individual genes (Dawkins 1989[1976]: x–xi). Yet it is striking in Dawkins' work how the metaphorical language he chooses appears loaded with particular kinds of assumptions about 'human females' and 'human males'. For instance, he outlines two strategies for mate selection in females of all species: the strategy of choosing a mate likely to assist with raising offspring he calls the 'domestic bliss' strategy and the strategy of choosing based on the quality of a mate's genetic material he calls the 'he-man' strategy. He suggests that 'human females [might] play the domestic-bliss rather than the he-man strategy', but appears to base this not on evidence but on the supposition that '[n]otions of females withholding copulation until a male shows some evidence of long-term fidelity may strike a familiar chord' (Dawkins 1989[1976]: 164). For a sociologist, the question is: with whom may these 'notions … strike a familiar chord' and why? This passage takes unpleasant stereotypes about women manipulatively holding back on having sex to 'catch' men and turns them into dubious 'familiar' knowledge about how women supposedly act. Of course, much of Dawkins's work is based on more careful interpretation of scientific evidence, and he is not suggesting that genes totally determine human ways of living but that which genetic tendencies 'win' is determined by the particular cultural context (Dawkins 1989[1976]: 164).

The importance of the social context and of the mutual forming of environment and genes by each other is found in more recent versions of sociobiology such as the Genetic-Social framework developed by Sibeon (2004) and extended by Owen (2013). However, their efforts to move away from the 'over-socialised' (or not biological enough) gaze on sexuality represented by Foucault (1990a) and Gagnon and Simon (2005 [1973]) are problematic. Owen (2013: 76) presents evidence of a gene that 'directly affects sexuality in human beings' but rather than linking this clearly back to the sexual drive, slides into explaining how if this gene is not operating then individuals do not go through puberty and if genetically male they look like girls. This appears to confuse sex (biological maleness), gender (expectations around masculinity) and sexuality (who you desire) in ways that sociologists have worked hard to avoid (West and Zimmerman 1987). Thus careful interpretation of scientific work is necessary for scientists and for social scientists, although this can be difficult for social scientists who may have limited knowledge or training in the hard sciences. More collaborative work crossing the science/social science boundary would be valuable in this respect, yet there are challenges sociologists can make using the tools of their own discipline.

Sociology can challenge the idea that sociobiology is a set of indisputable facts, and reveal that it is a way of thinking often utilised to conveniently reinforce dominant political models of people as possessive individuals. That dominant model of economic, rational individuals seeking to make the most of themselves has a particular history (MacPherson 1962). The dominant sociobiological interpretation of evolution emphasises the inevitability of 'selfish' competition between individuals or genes. One example of this is Tim Owen's (2013) criticism of the supposed 'essentialism' of many sociological explanations. There is some merit in Owen's call for sociologists to explore new evidence for a partly genetic basis to behaviour (see also Guo 2006; Bolhuis et al. 2011). However, in explaining the need to do this his criticism of sociology involves defining essentialism not as a belief that social groups or phenomena have 'real essences' or distinct intrinsic properties (Fuss 1990), but as 'the illegitimate attribution of homogeneity to social phenomena on a priori grounds' (Owen 2013: 73). There is a healthy body of work in sociology and especially feminism, which points out the flaws of over-generalising about social categories such as 'women' (see Crenshaw 1989; Yuval-Davis 2006), but this does not mean that to talk of any group of people *as a group* is to reduce them to an '*essentialist* monolithic block' (Owen 2013: 73, emphasis in the original). The implication appears to be that one can or should speak only of individuals (and their genes) in trying to explain behaviour. However, there are alternative views of genetic selection that recognise mutual aid as crucial in survival (Jackson and Rees 2007: 925–926). Some of the other problems biologists have noted with sociobiology arise from its way of treating behaviour as though it is a thing rather than a process, the grouping together of phenomena in arbitrary ways and the imposition of metaphors for human behaviour onto animals (Lewontin 1976). There is not scope to discuss all these here, but the last problem relates closely to new thinking about the relationship between human and non-human animals in recent years.

Human Animals

There is optimism to the way that studies of human-animal relations force re-examination of some of sociology's central assumptions about sociality and human dominance over other species. Extending the boundaries of sociology to include non-human animals highlights that society is not solely a human phenomenon. There has been relatively recent acknowledgement of how animals are used to feed, clothe, work for and entertain human beings (see Bryant 1979). Since then a growing number of scholars have challenged the exclusion of non-human animals from sociology (see for example Franklin 1999; Twine 2010; Wilkie 2010). Kay Peggs (2013) has convincingly argued that a focus on relations between human and non-human animals raises questions about what can be included in sociological inquiry. However, studies on non-human animals – even as they relate to humans – have been limited within sociology. This is partly because of distinctions sociologists make between humans and other animals, distinctions usually traced back to George Herbert Mead. Peggs (2013: 594–5) claims that Mead's position explicitly marks humans as superior. She questions Mead's (1962) arguments that sociology should not deal with non-human animals because they do not have language and lack shared meanings. She also questions whether humans alone produce a sense of self by orienting themselves to others. These arguments have become the 'traditional sociological point of view' (Peggs 2013: 595) and led to viewing non-human animals as instinctual and incapable of social complexity. Wilkie and McKinnon (2013) suggest, however, that tracing anthropocentric (human-centred) sociology back to Mead misrepresents his intellectual project and ignores elements of his work that may aid in exploring interspecies interactions. For example, they argue that Mead does not make a sharp distinction between humans and other animals but compares them in a continuum from more to less social. For Mead, cooperative versus non-cooperative relations are more of a divider. In such relations, gesture is important both for humans and animals. While vocal gestures allow for self-consciousness and complex sociality, this does not inevitably exclude non-human animals as they may 'do mind' without language. Mead himself discusses how birds imitate each other, thus calling forth the same response in the other as in the self and showing they can take the role of the other. Nevertheless, studies suggesting that non-human animals are 'minded' social agents are still questioned by many sociologists who claim that they are based on anthropomorphism. This means attributing human traits to animals in possibly unwarranted ways.

Sociologists, as touched on in the previous section, are also wary of related sociobiological arguments that human behaviour is instinctual and genetically driven just like in other species (Peggs 2013: 595–596). Animal and human societies are not the same, but neither are they completely distinct. Animals form part of human social activity, animals may have species-specific ways of being social and humans can interact in social ways with other animals (Wilkie 2015). However, human-animal studies somewhat overlook that the relationship between humans and animals can be highlighted not just by seeing animals as more human-like, but as Badiou (2001) does, by recognising the animality of humans. Such recognition can encourage further an optimism of the will in more seriously challenging the special status of humanity and taking a more humble position on our place on this earth.

Studying animal-human relations can also be optimistic in making a case for sociology as advocacy for oppressed groups (Peggs 2013). In this case, Peggs argues that sociologists can stand up for animals and protect them against mistreatment. This challenges those (such as Hammersley 1999; see also Chapter 6) who argue that sociology should describe society as it is, rather than advocate how it should be. Although Gouldner

(1970) does not endorse using sociology to speak for the interests of disadvantaged groups, Peggs supports his call for a reflexive sociology that recognises how values shape what sociologists study and how. She also draws on Mills's (1959) claim that sociology is the study of problems and that problems are entangled with values. However, to consider sociology as the study of social problems rather than social questions might promote a pathology of social life. Nevertheless, recognition of how values influence sociology can lead to questions of how sociology can influence values. Peggs is not the first to consider whether or not sociology does or 'should' involve supporting particular causes or groups. Those rallied under the flag of advocacy sociology by Peggs (2013: 599–600) include Burawoy (2005) with his public sociology, Dorothy Smith's (1987) sociology for women and much other feminist sociology. Howard Becker (1967) is also briefly claimed as a sympathiser keen for sociologists to declare whose side we are on. However, not all of Human Animal Studies takes an advocacy position and there are a range of other insights to be gained from a more multispecies approach (Wilkie 2015).

Critical optimism around animal-human relations can allow us to question whether social inequalities are related to biological differences (Peggs 2013: 596). To recognise non-humans as mindful actors extends the sociological imagination to animals. The animal protection movement has, for example, turned private troubles around animals into public issues. This may have political consequences but also tells us about the co-existence of social systems which treat animals as objects and goods, alongside people feeling that they should care for animals. Overall, there is strong evidence that how we think about and relate to animals is being re-evaluated in ways that show greater concern for non-human creatures (Wilkie 2015). This has implications for understanding human relations with a range of others as capable of taking less hierarchical forms.

In order to explore power and consider less hierarchical ways of relating it may be important sociologically to recognise the agency of non-human animals, but Wilkie (2015) argues that this needs to be done contextually. She suggests that previous thinking has acknowledged the symbolic importance of animals as represented by humans, but the emphasis has now shifted to the actual relationships between humans and animals. Actor Network Theory (ANT) has been one approach in making this shift. However, Wilkie (2015: 330) suggests that in its attention to the webs of relations and practices connecting humans and other animals, ANT loses sight of individual agency and tends to treat animals, humans and objects as though they are all the same. She proposes that what is required is 'a more contextualised understanding of interspecies relations that considers where species are located in a network and any power differentials that may exist' (Wilkie 2015: 330). A more contextual approach could address an issue which the study of animal-human relationships can highlight but often fails to examine; that is the specificity of human bodies as compared to animal bodies. Thus other areas such as the sociology of the body and the sociology of food may provide some important conceptual tools for further exploring the way in which human and other animals depend on each other and yet are distinct. The study of human-animal relations can also prompt thinking about how human beings are part of, not 'masters' of nature.

Nature, the Environment and Climate Change

In the face of the challenges posed by environmental problems there is urgent need to reconsider to what extent humans are free from dependence on or links to nature. A view of supposed human triumph over nature might be an understandable product of increasing technological capabilities, of twentieth century 'exuberance', and of sociological reactions to biological imperialism, but there was early sociological recognition of the need to accommodate natural logics. Weber and Durkheim arguably shared the belief that social reality should be explained in reference to social factors, without entirely dismissing the importance of the natural. Weber maintains a qualitative distinction between meaningless nature or instinct and meaningful human actions (Karakayali 2014: 5), but does acknowledge the limits and grounding of social and cultural life in the natural world (Albrow 1990: 257). Like Weber, Marx divides humans from non-human animals but also highlights that there is a two-way relationship between nature and humans. For example, in formulating the relationship between consciousness and the division of labour, Marx began by stating that an animal could not have 'relations' with anything because it is not conscious of its relations to others as relations. He says:

'it is consciousness of nature, which first appears to men as a completely alien, all-powerful and unassailable force, with which men's relations are purely animal and by which they are over-awed like beasts; it is thus a purely animal consciousness of nature (natural religion)'. (Marx 1983/1932: 174)

Within early social organisation, 'the restricted relation of men to nature determines their restricted relation to each other' (Marx 1983/1932: 174). As society becomes more complex through producing more things and people, the division of labour develops and eventually capitalism breaks the metabolic link between nature and labour, alienating individuals from their work, from the natural world and their sense of being human (Foster 1999; Marx 1959/1844). The metabolic link is one in which human embodied labour is connected to the rhythms of the natural world, its cycle of days and seasons. Industrialisation under capitalist control distances the bulk of humanity from these rhythms. Others like Murphy (1995) advocate sociological recognition of human activity as limited as well as enabled by the natural world. Thus social action must be situated in the context of natural *processes* rather than understandings entrenched within a nature versus nurture debate. This involves seeing the limits of human activity as dynamic not static and requires synthesis of sociological work on agency with theories about structure, according to Murphy. An example might be to see how climate change forces people to migrate because local social structures cannot sustain people in the face of worsening flooding (Black et al. 2011). This attention to structure may be evident in later sociological engagement with climate change, as we will see below, but the form of that engagement is of some concern.

If sociologists are to engage critically yet effectively with climate change debates, they must provide more than criticisms of Science. Some argue that what is required is a synthesis of natural and social science. Constance Lever-Tracy (2008) proposes that natural and social scientists must work together in multidisciplinary ways to solve such a complex problem, indicative of the intertwining of human sociality with its natural environment. Others suggest that her view of multidisciplinarity is too respectful of natural science and would leave sociologists in danger of reproducing the dominant discourse. Grundmann and Stehr (2010: 903) thus propose that an interdisciplinarity which makes use of a sociological framework is likely to be more efficacious. Both note the late arrival of sociologists to the issue of climate change, Lever-Tracy finding it hard to explain given global warming's potential impact on human lives and the kind of major changes in how we live that it is likely to entail. Grundmann and Stehr (2010) think it perhaps easier to explain if sociologists are given some credit for recognising the problems of criticising the construction of climate change debates, given that this could appear to give weight to climate change sceptics. Various other factors are identified to explain the lack of sociological attention to global warming such as an indifference towards the future in contemporary society coupled with sociological dislike of explaining social facts in naturalistic terms. Sociologists tend to also reject orientation to the long-term future as teleological, as though it is headed to a particular goal, and usually lack the ability to judge the validity of natural science claims for themselves. This has led them to avoid the issue and to continue to understand nature as stable background to society or as a social construction (Lever-Tracy 2008). However, it is also the case that the dominance of the natural sciences in framing how climate change is understood has made it difficult for sociologists to intervene in meaningful ways. The emphasis on modelling possible scenarios means that scientists wanting to include information about human behaviour want that information in forms that can be fitted into their models. Most sociologists resist the idea of modelling social processes in such ways (Grundmann and Stehr 2010: 901). Sociologists thus need to decide whether they want to lend support to sceptics by criticising the science, or to persuade scientists and publics that sociology has something different to offer in order to better understand how to prevent or ameliorate the worst effects arising from human impact on nature.

Aside from criticism of science, sociologists have been pessimistic about efforts to deal with climate change because they see them as problematically enhancing technocracy and big government and it is other social scientists like the geographer Swyngedouw (2010) who have offered alternatives. Anthony Giddens (2009) neglects even his own sociological conceptualising in *The Politics of Climate Change* in favour of a focus on policy (Grundmann and Stehr 2010: 906). John Urry (2008) does use sociology to provide thoughtful but not hopeful imaginings of the consequences of climate change, environmental degradation and resource depletion for human societies. He foresees two main possibilities: a violent society controlled by tribal warlords fighting over resources, or a digital panopticon in which mobility is tightly controlled, especially for those who are not members of the social elite. These 'bleak scenarios' (Urry 2008: 261) do at least give some attention to the unequal effects of threats to the environment. As Swyngedouw (2010: 221) argues, however, political recognition that 'the poor will be hit first and hardest by climate change' tends to be a populist ploy used to reinforce the global threat to all humans. This is hardly optimistic, although Swyngedouw (2010) does offer some cause for an 'optimism of the will' (Gramsci 1978/1929: 18) in his criticism of the apocalyptic terms in which climate change is presented. This mode of presentation involves using fear to control; managing fear being key to the politics of capitalism (Badiou 2007). Thus a questioning of capitalism can arise from social scientific understandings of climate change.

A sociology of climate change can be optimistic about the potential of human beings to live differently, in ways other than via capitalistic exploitation of people and natural resources. Challenges to capitalism do occur within environmental sociology, which might not seem an obvious place for optimism. Debates within the sociology of the environment are between the ecological modernisers (see Mol and Sonnenfeld 2000) and the eco-Marxists or eco-socialists (see Buttel et al. 2002; Huan 2010). The former assume that technological change will allow adaptation to climate change and a reduction of its effects and see possibility in forms of green capitalism such as carbon trading. Eco-Marxists suggest that a much more fundamental change in our way of life is required, one which challenges capitalism and consumerism (Lever-Tracy 2008). Living differently might involve less waste, more sustainable use of resources and more equal distribution of goods and this might require a different kind of economy not oriented to profit making. However, ecosociology has emerged, drawing principally on critical realism, questioning the overly materialist bias of eco-Marxism. It is not simply the material or economic conditions that determine how people are able to live, but nor is it just ideas that construct social reality. Ecosociologists argue that eco-Marxist and constructivist positions tend to decentre human beings in thinking about the natural world, rather than thinking about environmental issues in terms of how they impact on human health and well-being as well as looking at how humans impact on the environment (Vaillancourt 1995; 2010). Perhaps decentring *individuals* is more the issue.

Social scientists can move climate change debates forward by providing a view of people as vulnerable and dependent on their relations with others. This counters dominant models of humans as autonomous individuals. The optimism here lies in the possibilities arising from letting go of fantasies of controlling nature. Nigel Clark (2011: 57) recognises the asymmetrical relation of humans to the earth and attends to the body 'as site of impingement of forces beyond its control'. His book *Inhuman Nature* contains an especially interesting chapter where he uses Levinas to focus on human enjoyment of the earth and how this is disrupted by a natural disaster like the 2004 Boxing Day tsunami. Clark acknowledges criticisms of responses to the tsunami. Spending and aid efforts were excessive and poorly directed, the role of poor infrastructure in worsening the effects of the disaster for the poorest members of society was ignored. However, he notes the failure of such criticisms to recognise aspects of human vulnerability (Clark 2011: 66). His focus is on how people were thrown together as a result of the tsunami so that capitalist models of tourism based on exchange fell apart. Locals took tourists in and looked after them, tourists helped with the cleaning up and 'another kind of being with others emerged' (Clarke 2011: 59). This calls to mind some of the insights from the study of human–animal relations challenging beliefs in human hierarchical control over nature. It also echoes the discussion in Chapter 8 about the need for an ethic of social flesh in which care for others and for the planet requires a recognition of vulnerability and interdependence. This may require questioning capitalism as 'the end of history' (Fukuyama 1992) and recognising alternative worldviews and possibilities for living and relating which are less destructive of the natural environment.

Indigenous worldviews are one resource for appreciating and mending the vital relationship between humans and their natural environment. Non-Western thinking has a much richer tradition of thinking about, for example, the connection of human being to the land (Connell 2007: 195–209; Tuhiwai-Smith 1999). Without romanticising this connection, there may be things to learn, not least about the damaging impact of unbridled development on people (Sampson 2015). There is beginning to be some recognition of how indigenous knowledge and practices might, for instance, provide information about how to mitigate and adapt to climate change (for example, Green and Raygorodetsky 2010; Nyong et al. 2007). One example is how peoples of the Sahel in Africa have used strategies of soil conservation, forest and crop management and cultivation and preservation of biodiversity in ways that mitigate the climate change they experience in the form of worsening droughts. They also adapt to these droughts via strategies of emergency fodder use, keeping varied livestock, culling the weaker ones when water is short and engaging in nomadic mobility to wetter areas. Whilst the details of these strategies might be context specific, they indicate the sophisticated and appropriate potential of indigenous knowledge to provide ways of tackling climate change that enhance community, belonging and stability. Such approaches can also offer more participatory responses to climate change that share sustainable development concerns with economy, equity and environment and involve communities (Nyong et al. 2007). Some indigenous people may question the extent to which indigenous knowledge and practices are always participatory and inclusively equitable (for example, Szászy 1993), and there are examples like Easter Island where indigenous practices may have contributed to ecodisaster (but see Rainbird 2002). Nevertheless, indigenous knowledge can offer viable alternatives to some of the limitations of 'Western' practices of relating to the natural world. Working with communities and recognising their indigenous knowledge about their environment is key to formulating effective responses to climate change in the places and amongst the peoples most urgently affected.

Conclusion

Optimism is important in appreciating how human related destruction of the natural environment has prompted a rethink of the relationship between people and nature. Sociology has tended to bracket off nature, partly to distinguish itself as a discipline, but partly to avoid the pessimistic flaws of biological reductionism. Sociology is, for instance, critical of sociobiology for tending to justify inequalities rather than question them or consider how they can change. Sociobiology also typically ignores social complexity and sometimes wanders from the scientific evidence in its focus on the drive to reproduce as explaining human behaviour. It is a view of the world that is socially and politically located and tends to be influenced by dominant ideas about the centrality of individuals. Other scientists point out the importance of mutual cooperation in evolutionary survival.

There are more optimistic ways to engage with the relationship between nature and humanity, as evident in the way that the study of human-animal relations can reorient sociology towards new understandings of sociality and of human dominance. Human-animal studies also encourages an optimistic view of sociology as able to advocate for oppressed groups and help improve their status. This area of study puts into question the idea of social inequalities as the inevitable result of 'natural' differences. A contextualised recognition of the agency of animals can assist in exploring how power can be challenged and highlight human dependence on, rather than mastery of, the natural world. These insights are useful if also extended to debates around climate change. The current and likely future state of the environment suggests that sociology cannot maintain an illusion of human control over nature. Sociologists need to make contributions to climate change debates that go beyond being critical of the science or of the way that proposed solutions might allow governments too much control over citizens. Sociological contributions to this debate can offer optimistic challenges to capitalist structures and prompt thought about different ways of living. In doing so sociologists can remind us of human embodied vulnerability and our dependence on other humans, animals and the natural world. The trick is to keep in mind the possibilities for change that look beyond capitalism, that appreciate what human solidarity can do and that incorporate alternative worldviews contained, for example, in indigenous knowledge. Critical optimism in this sphere is not an intellectual luxury but a pressing necessity.

ACTIVITY

In groups, come up with three suggestions for living more sustainably. How could we use less energy by changing the way we live? Who have you suggested should make changes? How would changes be enforced?

OR: Discuss pets you have owned. What kind of relationship did/do you have with them? How much control do you have over their lives? Should *they* have more control? Why or why not?

ENCHANTMENT

Every August there is an international festival in Edinburgh featuring classical music, dance and theatre and accompanied by a fringe festival stuffed with the latest comedy shows, experimental theatricals, circuses, and all kinds of singing, dancing and other creative performances. On my way to work it is not unusual to see people who seem to be dressed as abstract vegetables, or someone carrying a 'guitar' made out of balloons. From my office I can hear a troupe of drummers followed by a slightly off key singer performing U2 covers. At lunchtime I can pop out to see anything from a talented bunch of youngsters improvising a new Jane Austen novel, to a performance of Antigone, to the amazing bubbleman. Every night, assuming I am back in time from the symphony orchestra concert, or comedy show, I can watch fireworks over the castle from the comfort of my own kitchen. It is, in short, a magical time. It is also busy and noisy and hard to get around the city. The sometimes weird shows are packed into a precisely timetabled programme and only impressive organisation makes it all work so that fun is possible and the city can cope with the huge influx of people. Yet it can be enchanting.

Enchantment is a process via which ideas, beliefs and practices lift people and their activities out of the routine and give them a sense of specialness, of delight, of meaning. An understanding of enchantment is key to imagining and enacting alternative visions of social life. To focus on enchantment is to challenge Weber's (1970/1948) view of modernity as characterised by rationalisation processes that disenchanted the world, confined human thought and creativity and left us praying to the Gods of money and reason. Superstition, magic and religion supposedly no longer shaped how the world was understood. Yet Weber continued to see that ideas, beliefs and meaning were central to social life and that rationalisation had positive aspects. This chapter is optimistic in examining how people draw on beliefs, meanings, memories and imagination in finding meaningful ways to live together. In contrast to Weber there are those who claim that processes of re-enchantment are observable in modernity. Jenkins (2000) for example, contests whether disenchantment is as universal and on-going a process as Weber suggested and Ritzer (2010) has explored contemporary efforts to enchant the world through spectacular and simulated forms of consumption. I do not propose a re-enchanting of a disenchanted world, but question the completeness of disenchanting processes and seek to explore where remaining or new sources of magic and mystery may lie.

Still Enchanted? Religion

Disenchantment processes are not complete. Weber (1970/1948: 129–56, 267–301) argued that spaces for enchantment disappear as modernity sees reason replace religion, magic and superstition in making sense of the world. It has become 'a world robbed of Gods' (Weber 1970/1948: 282). He may not have been entirely pessimistic in his appreciation of the complexity of social change, which noted the gifts as well as difficulties brought by modernising processes (Jenkins 2000: 11). However, his overall assessment of the disenchantment of modernity is that it imprisons and constrains individuals and renders their lives less meaningful. This happens through processes of rationalisation and bureaucratisation but also through processes of secularisation.

Yet disenchantment in the form of the secularisation of Western populations has been contested. Dropping adherence to religion in the latter twentieth century has been clear according to Steve Bruce (for example, 2002). He takes secularisation to have meant a decline in the authority of religious beliefs and in the social significance of religion. Empirical data, such as on falling church attendance, appeared to support the idea that fewer people make organised religion a central or even important feature of their lives. Yet others such as Rodney Stark (1999) disputed much of this evidence and argued that secularisation assumed past levels of faith not borne out by historical evidence and that the practices of late twentieth century people did not support the secularisation thesis. Grace Davie (2001) was more equivocal about whether or not a clear secularisation process was at work, or whether things like lower church attendance were part of a shift towards believing without belonging. In other words, people may still have some kind of religious faith but may not join any kind of religious group. More recently, however, there has been an apparent 'resurgence of religion'. This is partly an artefact of migration, as the West has become home to ethnic immigrants for whom religion remains a guiding principle. New questions are thus raised about the relationship between being secular and being modern (Davie 2013).

Both new tensions and possibilities arise around religion as a source of enchantment that might challenge, not just enhance the social order. As a form of individual salvation religion can rescue individuals from the banality of everyday life, but as a form of belonging it might create new social problems. One example is British teenagers leaving their suburban bedrooms to join the Islamic State in Syria (Bakker and de Leede 2015). Tensions emerge when the expectation is that 'good' citizens demonstrate loyalty to a secular state which fails to aid, or actively harms 'brothers and sisters' in the faith by bombing Afghanistan or Syria. A cause like *jihad* or assistance with humanitarian efforts in Islamic nations might give some Moslem people, like these teenagers, a sense of purpose in contrast to the mundane context and constraints of their lives in Britain where their identities are questioned and often devalued (Bakker and de Leede 2015). In this case it links young Moslems into a sense of nation and common purpose elsewhere, but challenges the social order in Britain. Their enchantment is perceived as problematic within a modern secular state where formal religion is not expected to give meaning to people's lives in these ways and a diversity of forms of disenchantment are encouraged.

Formal religion may no longer have a monopoly on individual enchantment, but the plurality of routes to transcending the mundane does not mean that enchantment is inevitably individualised and thus disempowering. Sloterdijk (2013) has suggested that more diversity in practising forms of self-improvement may allow for greater freedom of expression and for societies which encourage the full development of human capabilities. He tends to focus on forms of practising oriented towards pushing at the limits of human abilities such as being elite athletes or tightrope walkers and his vision favours individual improvement over more collective or political forms of change. Sloterdijk (2013) sees the negotiation of hierarchies as key to these forms of improvement and appears to valorise forms of self-reliance and overcoming of adversity which fit conveniently with ideals of neo-liberal individuals who exercise choice.

In contrast Foucault's (1990b) historical analysis of forms of self-care tends more towards a critical evaluation of how processes of power produce such disciplined individuals. Although Foucault's examples are of how individuals in Ancient Greece practised ways of looking after their bodies and souls, those practices are thought of in much more relational ways than Sloterdijk so they include how elite Greek men aimed to improve the self through the marital role or within their political careers or in their sexual relationships with boys. Arguably his earlier work (Foucault 1979) suggests that modern forms of power begin to sepa-rate off individuals from each other as they internalise discourses about 'normal' bodies and ways of behaving and work on themselves to fit with these norms. Relations to others are acknowledged, but the more collective aspects of self-care are not thoroughly considered by Foucault (1990b). However, his ideas can help us see that current practices of self-care might not just isolate and disempower individuals but be ways in which they resist domination and find meaning and delight. This is done by transforming the kinds of selfhood available to themselves and others. One example might be the ways in which for women with disabilities doing physical activity is a form of self-care but if politicised it can also transform for the better commonly held negative ideas about people with disabilities as a group (Guthrie and Castelnuovo 2001). Thus, indi-viduals might be understood as constrained in similar ways to Weber's moderns who are limited by the hard shell of bureaucratised life, but as able to resist. People can transform the social world through meaningful forms of self-care that, in certain contexts, can bring not just individual change but wider transformation. This suggests that a pessimistic view of disenchanting produces an incomplete vision of social change.

More Enchanting Activities: Special Practices on Holiday

There is some cause for optimism in the array of extra-ordinary activities through which current seeking after enchantment is pursued. Celebrating special occasions or 'traditional' rituals, nationalism and remembrance (Hobsbawm and Ranger 1983; West 2015), music or art (Malhotra 1979; Young 2014) and extreme sports (Wheaton 2004), to name a few. Typically these ways of finding some occasional magic and meaning in life are noted as temporary and while an escape for some, are argued to be a trap for others (Skeggs 2004: 49). The example I will discuss here is holidays. Going on holiday in another country may open people up to new exciting experiences and different cultures. However, it can reinforce the marginality of the people from cultures under the 'tourist gaze', who have to make their living by performing to travellers easily digestible versions of their culture in the form of traditional dances or special rituals (Chan 2014). Meanwhile, there are also other local people doing the far from enchanting mundane work of cleaning hotel rooms, serving drinks and waiting tables (Urry and Larsen 2011: 75–97). And even for those privileged enough to be enjoying a holiday, mass tourism can make the reality far from the magical experience imagined. A lot of contemporary tourism is packaged in very predictable, large scale ways which can make it a lot like a McDonald's hamburger: you know what you are going to get but it is not very special (Ritzer 2010, Ritzer and Liska 1997). Thus many tourists find that instead of a hoped for special moment on a deserted beach or strolling through some ancient ruins, they find themselves fighting with hundreds of others for a stretch of sand or sharing the ruins with large tour parties loudly discussing where they are going for lunch. There are also forms of packaged holiday leisure like theme parks which rather than offering freedom and authentic experiences of nature or other cultures, are highly simulated and predictable. Disneyland can offer some enchantment, but may not feel very like 'the magic kingdom' when you are in a two hour queue for a ride, seeing the same performance by Mickey Mouse every half hour and you realise the big tree you are staring at is made of plastic (Bryman 2004; Ritzer 2010). Although these criticisms of the exploitation and profit-centred nature of much mass tourism are warranted, this can seem an instance of sociologists ruining everybody's fun. A degree of optimism is required.

Some degree of critical optimism about the vitality of extra-ordinary activities such as holidays can examine how they might offer forms of enchantment by introducing large numbers of people to different ways of life (Rojek 2000: 65–6). It is not insignificant that travel and tourism are now open to many more people than in the past, they have been democratised. Prior to the nineteenth century, travelling any distance for leisure was only really available to the male elites in Europe, who from the seventeenth to nineteenth centuries routinely took the Grand Tour of the key capitals and ancient sites as a cap to their education (Urry and Larsen 2011). As industrialisation speeded up during the nineteenth century, new concentrations of people in crowded and dirty cities, plus new technologies like trains and aeroplanes, gradually made holidays more appealing and possible for people other than the very wealthy. Some may bemoan the way that mass tourism dulls the magic aura of places by filling them with crowds from all walks of life, but this can fail to question the elitism and exclusion attached to maintaining 'specialness'. As Rojek (2000) notes, a focus on disenchantment fails to acknowledge how going on holiday might help people learn about other cultures and how this might translate into the development and acceptance of multi-culturalism or even fostering new transnational cultures. People take home with them a new appreciation of other kinds of people, other ways of dressing and eating that can contribute to making their home society more multi-cultural and potentially more tolerant of difference. However, as well as an appreciation of difference, tourism may encourage transnational forms of culture which are not so linked to particular places but make accessible a shared sense of world heritage through sights like the Eiffel Tower or the Pyramids of Egypt. This is not to neglect the kitsch or commodified nature of much tourism, of which tourists are often well aware, but to remember some of its potentially positive aspects.

In searching for critically optimistic possibilities for special activities to be enchanting, it is argued that those which are less commodified in packaged ways and less exploitative of host peoples are more likely to give people a real sense of meaning. However, it is not easy to escape commodification and packaging as has been evident in volunteering holidays. These are where Westerners now often pay so that they can go and offer their usually unskilled labour to charities in developing countries who struggle to make use of it without incurring costs (Hindman 2014). Nevertheless, it is argued that volunteer tourism and other ethical alternatives to mainstream tourism can contribute to the development of more sustainable forms of tourism in developing nations. That at least these forms of ecotourism may have positive as well as negative consequences for the host society. Ecotourism as an ideology, and sometimes as practice, can challenge unbridled profit motives and harmful development and allow less exploitative kinds of relationships between tourists and their hosts, as well as between tourists and the environment. They can also can give travellers a sense of freedom from the constraints and problems of their everyday life back home, and for some provide highly meaningful, even 'spiritual' experiences (Duffy 2002). Special activities are, however, just that and people cannot engage in them all the time so they might seek enchanting on a more regular basis.

Regular Enchantment: Imagination

Imagination is a rather sociologically neglected area of life that may offer more regular, but not inevitably subversive, enchanting possibilities. There is remarkably little attention to imagination and fantasy as social phenomena (Cohen and Taylor 1992: 90). What little there is does not offer an optimistic view. When Stanley Cohen and Laurie Taylor (1992: 88) try to get to grips with 'the mental magic of fantasy' in exploring *Escape Attempts* from everyday life, they conclude that fantasy tends rather to support than subvert bureaucratised, paramount reality. It does so because individual fantasies are drawn from a fairly small and predictable cultural pool of themes. In some quarters fantasising may be thought immoral, for example within Catholicism, as it lets in 'evil thoughts'. Other ideas based on Freud suggest that it is an acceptable way to find some satisfaction or relief from the everyday. Yet it can help shore up the status quo by helping people cope with boring tasks and drab lives. Cohen and Taylor (1992: 99–101) identify a variety of forms of daydreaming that keep people tied to life as it is. There are starter fantasises to help people get going. We might imagine an action-filled day ahead to help us get out of bed. Stopper fantasies will delay or prevent certain actions, for example academics might imagine a long journey, boring dinner and poor accommodation to stop themselves accepting a lecture invitation. Then there are maintainer fantasies to keep people going. They might include the kinds of elaborate games that factory workers invent to help them pass the time doing dull, routine jobs (Burawoy 1979; Roy 1960).

A sociology for optimists might acknowledge that fantasies are institutionalised because they offer support for enduring reality but would also explore further imaginings as resistance to social control. Our inner life is not a free space of creativity according to Cohen and Taylor. Society 'regulates and shapes the nature of that inner life' (Cohen and Taylor 1992: 105). The resources to indulge fantasies are arguably more readily available than in the past because they can be accessed through mass culture (Cohen and Taylor 1992: 102–103). This does not mean that there is more freedom, it means that our fantasies are even more ready-made products unlikely to challenge how the world works. Cohen and Taylor (1992: 105–107) note that fantasies are unreliable, that they elevate routine experiences and are difficult to control and often of short duration. What they fail to consider is that although fantasies are unreliable in that we cannot conjure them when we wish, this could make them less open to commercial appropriation and indeed their unpredictability is something that could make them a good counterpoint for the predictability of bureaucratised life. When they can be summoned, the break from the routine that they provide is potentially an important source of meaning for people in their everyday lives, even if it does not effect wider change. And the difficulty of controlling and keeping fantasies alive may be part of their allure. Slipping in and out of daydreams may be a way to rest weary minds, over-stimulated by modern life (Simmel 1950/1908). Certainly these possibilities seem worthy of further sociological research to examine more fully the importance of such imaginings.

Theoretically there is no inevitable connection between imagination and the reproduction of current unequal power relations. Carol Smart (2007: 49–52) has given some attention to the crucial role of the imaginary in relationships. How we feel about others is linked with social changes and social meanings. For example, ideals of family life play their part in how we do family and how we feel about how we do it. The rituals and stories that constitute meanings about families and relationships tell us a good deal about what matters to people, but can also sediment constraints and inequalities. However, in reflecting on the imaginary we can move between what matters to people and very broad cultural concerns. In doing so there are insights to be gained about everyday life and about how it is imbued with meaning. For example, the daily working of family life does not automatically reproduce capitalist relations of exploitation. This insight can be extended to other social phenomena.

One source of daydreams and imaginings apparently typical of twenty-first century life is celebrity, but this is not considered a cause for optimism about less hierarchical societies. If people imagine themselves as or with celebrities, if celebrities are thus the model of all that is exciting and glamorous and sought after, this seems to make them enchanting, but as new Gods or new aristocracy. Yet the importance of celebrity in modern life can communicate other things about what matters to people and what is socially significant. In what might seem obsessive levels of interest in not always very famous people, it is possible to trace forms of imagined connection to others in a diverse and often fragmented world. Celebrity society may be an imagining of power, acted out in hierarchical ways like a new version of the court society that surrounded kings and queens (Van Kriekan 2012). This and many analyses of the cult of celebrity assume it is fundamentally individualistic and narcissistic. Celebrity in this vision simply reinforces inequalities and imagining a celebrity life is seen as another doomed escape attempt, shoring up the status quo rather than challenging it. However, it is possible to see interest in celebrity as based on love and as about developing a relationship (even if imagined) with a loved character (Illouz 2009: 395). Many young people may find connections with celebrities meaningful, for example, many see celebrities as more authentic, open and trustworthy than politicians in discussing social and political issues (Manning et al. 2015). To only see imaginings related to celebrity as pathology or commodity (Ferris 2007), or as Van Kriekan does as reinforcing hierarchies of inequality, is to miss the meaningful part such imaginings can sometimes play in making people feel connected to others.

There are some indications that imaginings can provide meaning, that they do not only reinforce the stranglehold of reality but can be used in shaping social lives. Margaret Archer (2010: 282) argues that 'imagination plays a major role in realizing our commitments' via what Peirce calls 'preparatory meditation'. In other words, our agency, our sense of self and our actions are fundamentally shaped by various forms of thinking through and rehearsing future conversations and actions. Archer takes Peirce's version of the internal conversation as one way in which this is done. I might, for example, try to decide about breaking up with my boyfriend or girlfriend by playing out the conversation around 'going our separate ways' in my head. Thus imagining different selves and ways of living and relating to others is a mainstay of the reflexivity at the centre of making our way through the world and is part of how the social is reproduced. Yet as imaginings of this nature inform agency, there is no inevitability of conservation to this reproduction and it also involves change. Imagination can play a role in whether change is a tinkering around the edges of social life, or constitutes more transformative alteration.

Critical optimism about the role of imagination in transformatively enchanting the social in transforming ways can usefully borrow Cornelius Castoriadis's concept of the social imaginary. He defines the social imaginary as:

> the unceasing and essentially *undetermined* (social-historical and psychical) creation of figures/forms/images, on the basis of which alone there can ever be a question *of* 'something'. What we call 'reality' and 'rationality' are its works. (Castoriadis 1987: 3, emphasis in original)

In other words, we individually and collectively use our imaginings to create social life. Although rationalisation is supposedly the key character of the modern world, 'the modern world is just as dependent on the imaginary as any archaic or historical culture' (Castoriadis 1987: 156). He sees rationality itself as a form of the imaginary – it is an illusion or even a delusional pursuit of technical and economic development with no real end. Rather than actual needs, present social formations serve manufactured needs, needs imagined within the logic of the capitalist system. The individual is also treated within such systems as if they are purely mechanical and 'this is not less but *more* imaginary than claiming to see him [or her] as an owl' (Castoriadis 1987: 157). And alongside the market the other central institutional structure in modern life, the bureaucratic institution, is thoroughly imbued by the imaginary. Its self-referential pseudo-rationality is argued to bear no relation to social reality, but only to serve effectiveness, to aid 'growth' – asking no questions about effective for what or whom, growth for what end? This is a fundamentally different view from Weber's, even if Weber does recognise the importance of ideas in shaping the world. If the world is constituted by imagination, if it is not disenchanted but made through human creativity, it can be changed to accord more with the desires and dreams of individuals as they actively constitute their social context. Theoretically this has potential, but how imagination makes social life also needs empirical investigation.

How forms of optimistic imagining can work as sources of enchantment that can change lives is evident in research on people who migrate to find a better life. One of the issues with how concepts of the social imaginary are used is that they typically treat the social imaginary as a noun, a thing, rather than as a practice (O'Reilly 2014). By focusing on imaginings it is possible to appreciate how aspects of structure are internalised in a variety of ways and enacted according to the power and privilege of individuals and groups. This allows us to see how imaginings of a better life, well-illustrated in empirical studies of lifestyle migration done by O'Reilly, draw on and become social norms and are shaped by the social position of particular groups of migrants. Whether British migrants can match reality to their imagined expectations of a slower, more peaceful, more communal life in Spain or Malaysia, for instance, is largely a matter of the resources they can muster to make their experiences fit with the cultural imaginings about those places on which their decision to move is partly based. If they have enough money and can buy a comfortable house in a quiet village and retire to a life of ease involving regular interaction with those (usually other ex-patriots) living nearby, they are more likely to feel that their new life is close to what they hoped and dreamed. What they hoped and dreamed is based largely on the common meanings circulating about what a new life in Spain or Malaysia would be like. Yet if imagining is an on-going socially constituting process there is no inevitable determination of how people will relate to a place and the dominant imaginings can be contested and reshaped. Thus, imaginings as practices are both structural and creative (O'Reilly 2014). Such thinking could help contest whether 'escape' from paramount reality is the way to think about people's search for enchantment, or whether it is only by recognising the interlacing of structure and agency that a critically optimistic view of enchantment can be developed. In such a view, the very separation of enchanted spaces as though they are special comes under question, as we can see by moving on to discussion about love as a form of enchantment.

Everyday Enchanting Love?

It is suggested that within modernity romantic love and sex became separated off as a special site of excitement, of life-enriching enchantment. Love became like a new form of religion, a kind of 'secular salvation'

(Illouz 1998: 176). Weber (1970/1948: 343–350) himself noted how in the disenchanted world love became seen as an escape from the routine and rational by connecting people with 'real' feeling. Yet, not only are there problems with demarcating 'real' from 'false' feelings, but seeing emotions as enchanted also problematically opposes the 'free' space offered by love, to the constraints of rationality. This opposition between emotions and reason has been challenged by both feminists and neuro-scientists who affirm the intertwining of feeling and thinking (Damasio 2000; Jaggar 1990). Others question whether love really escapes ration-alisation or is itself subject to processes of regulation, ordering and commercialisation (Campbell 1987; Hochschild 2003). Yet these criti-cally pessimistic accounts fail to appreciate the ways in which love can be actively used as a resource to make life more meaningful.

If love does provide some spaces for enchantment this may bring positive change, for instance, allowing women to enjoy some forms of power over men and not simply to be oppressed by discourses or prac-tices around love. Heterosexual women are able to actively use romance narratives as a resource to make sense of their world. The perceived supe-rior emotional literacy of women can also contribute to making love a realm in which they can exercise a degree of control over supposedly emotionally unskilled men (Jackson 1993: 216). There are nevertheless dangers in acceding to these emotional stereotypes, in that they may in other ways perpetuate gender inequalities and fail to prompt men to take more responsibility for emotion work and other forms of care. However, if men are enchanted by love, they may be prompted towards changing in ways that might facilitate more equitable heterosexual relationships (Holmes 2015). Rather than more enchantment for men, there are argu-ably better possibilities offered by a more universal disenchantment of *romantic* love. Over-exposure to mass media discourses of love may make it difficult to have an innocent belief in love without reproducing cli-chés, but less intense investment in romantic love may promote recogni-tion of the sustaining importance of more everyday, 'comfortable' forms of love between partners (Illouz 1998). Illouz seems doubtful that this will happen, but recent empirical work has highlighted the importance of small acts of love and kindness in sustaining both love relationships between couples and wider networks of love and support (Brownlie 2014; Gabb and Fink 2015; Holmes 2014: 126). The mundane magic of less dramatic forms of love is worth considering.

Critical optimism can challenge views of the world as disenchanted by looking beyond romantic, to other forms of love. Sociology has had relatively little to say about romantic love (Jackson 1993), and even less about other forms such as parental, sibling or 'brotherly' love. Much of the literature on parenting deals rather indirectly with the love of parents for children (Jamieson 1998: 43–74) and almost never is parental love considered as a site of everyday enchantment. Gabb (2011) is one exception, capturing something of this with great sensitivity in some parents' descriptions of a special embodied emotional closeness they find when sharing a bath with their children. Love as a potentially enchanting lived experience between siblings is even more rarely studied (Mauthner 2005). In broader terms, it might be expected that sociologists would have an interest in 'brotherly' love given the reliance of much of the rhetoric of social order upon it (see Pateman 1988). Yet the experience of such love has also been little explored in its own right. Weber (1970/1948: 343–350) does note how the protestant religions in particular preached the need to subdue animal passions and instead focus on neighbourly or brotherly love. He explains how modern views of love as an overwhelming sensation conflicted with religious views of it as something that should be controlled and diffused. Thus, love for one's neighbour, or 'brotherly' love, was counter-posed to the unruly lustful passion of romantic love, thought to threaten rationally regulated marriage. Weber (1970/1948: 348) himself champions the possibilities of an ethic of brotherly love, over the supposedly selfish dangers of eroticism. Nevertheless he recognises eroticism as a way in which people may give their life meaning in ways that resemble or even replace religion. For him eroticism has the potential 'to mitigate modern disenchantment' at an individual, or dyadic level, but troubles social order more generally because it involves escape from everyday life at the expense of others (Shilling and Mellor 2010: 442, 446). Shilling and Mellor (2010) look for more collective, interdependent models of eroticism within the work of French feminists such as Cixous, Irigaray, and Kristeva. However, this leaves questions about the importance of 'neighbourly' love (a less gendered term than 'brotherly') as a source of collective meaning in a world somewhat de-articulated from traditional religion. This would seem a more likely source of interdependent and life-affirming forms of love.

It is important to consider neighbourly love as a form of enchantment because it highlights that collective forms of interdependence offer socially and not just individually transformative possibilities. It has been argued that different versions of neighbourly love, of 'brotherliness', emerge from Weber's sociology of religion, that not all are equally collectively oriented and most are not aimed at changing the world (Symonds and Pudsey 2006). However, in transference beyond religion, Weber (1970/1948: 343–350) recommends love for one's fellow humans as the basis of ethical conduct in pursuing politics or science as vocations. Certainly forms of neighbourliness appear to offer some connection beyond the self, they offer more than just the individual temporary relief from everyday routine that constitute most of the escape attempts described by Stan Cohen and Laurie Taylor (1992). There is little specifically written about such love, so there is room for more work on the topic. Although it may not be termed as such, arguably neighbourly love is the topic of much sociology under the rubric of 'community' or 'social movements'. It might be worth the labour of thinking about what such a form of love has and can do in the world. Space is limited here, but some examples come to mind. The abolition of slavery was achieved partly by claiming love for slaves as fellow human beings. Shared 'sisterly' love for other women was a key foundation for the feminist movement. Solidarity has been key to working-class politics. Of course, it can be argued that these examples of shared love for other humans barely existed in rhetoric, let alone reality. The very real achievements which accompanied them should, however, be a reminder that neighbourly love is not simply a bolster for social order but can provide a foundation for social alterations that favour greater equality. Thus, we have seen that exploring different forms of love as an everyday site of enchantment helps highlight the usefulness of a critically optimistic approach.

Conclusion

By engaging critical optimism it is possible to understand that the world has kept some enchantment, and there are new ways in which people find meaning and sometimes delight in their lives. Thus, although there has been a degree of disenchantment, as Weber so cogently argued, the processes of rationalisation he outlined have not been complete and total. There has even been contestation of the extent of the disenchantment associated with secularisation, as the retreat from traditional religious practice and belief has not included everyone everywhere. Religion remains an important source of meaning for many and can provide release from everyday banality, without inevitably shoring up the social order. However, other forms of enchantment have burgeoned. This does not mean that enchantment has become individualised and some of these forms can connect people to others and can play a part in potentially positive social transformation.

Important new forms of extra-religious enchantment that occur occasionally would benefit from the application of optimism to understanding them. The example of holidays was given, where critical optimism acknowledges that holidays can at least introduce people to different ways of life and this can bring changes in their home country given that holidays are no longer only accessible to rich elites. Such exposure to difference can, for example, encourage multiculturalism as well as a sense of shared global culture. It may be that there is more enchantment and more social and traveller benefits attached to certain kinds of holidays such as those which are less commercial and less exploitative of host nations and peoples.

Aside from these special occasions on which enchantment might be expected, there is also a need to be critically optimistic about more regular, everyday enchantment available through the imagination, although this may not be inevitably subversive. There is a need for more research about how the imagination might help in resisting social control. Theoretically, the imaginary is a useful concept in seeing that the imagination does not inevitably reproduce relations of domination. Imaginings associated with celebrity for example, do not only inscribe new social hierarchies but can be important, if fictive, ways to connect to others, based on love. Imagination is also an important element of agency, and thus used to shape lives. It is possible to see that it is part of wider social transformations, if we consider the social imaginary as describing the ways in which human dreams and desires actively constitute the social context. Imagination can effect a transforming enchantment of everyday lives, as was illustrated with respect to research on migration showing that imaginative practices are both structurally constrained and yet creative: they make lives. Other sources of everyday enchantment might include love. In its 'special' or romantic heterosexual and queer forms, love can bring shifts in relations of domination. It can allow women to exercise a degree of power, or men to shift towards more equitable ways of doing intimacy. Ways of loving can be queered or happily messed up by going beyond heterosexuality. Yet more sustainably and routinely enchanting might be non-romantic forms of love such as neighbourly love. There people may find meaning and delight in connection to others in ways that can foster change and promote greater equality in social life. So spaces for enchantment are imagined, felt and made through activity and through interaction. A sociology for optimists can illuminate the potential for enchantment as ever present within the social world.

ACTIVITY

Talk about what you imagine your life will be like in ten years. Do you like imagining this? Do you have different versions, some of which you find more realistic than others? What sort of world do you imagine you will be living in? How do your imaginings help you with your daily life now?

9

OPTIMISM

There are days when I think that if coining a collective noun one might speak of us as a pessimism of sociologists. A tendency to imagine the worst is not unwarranted, especially in a time of austerity, worldwide conflict and massive challenges like climate change and widening inequalities.[1] It might appear almost offensive to suggest that what we need is more optimism. However, in advocating the need for optimism I am certainly not arguing that individual positive thinking is the answer to what are thorny structural problems (see Ehrenreich 2009). Nor am I recommending positive psychology, the very name of which implies that the rest of the discipline focuses on the pathological. I am questioning whether optimists are thought terribly nice, but a little bit dim. Being clever and critical is often associated with elaborating what is wrong with the world, whereas optimism is typically thought naïve at best and complacent or stupid at worst (Tallis 1997: 180). Yet optimism need not entail a rejection of pessimism, it can 'simply be born of the prospects, excitement, and enjoyment of life' (Gouldner 1970: 434).

As sociologists, it is important to understand the role of optimism in people's lives. The relationship of optimism to feelings of happiness and hope is not very clear and warrants further research. Sociology is arguably guilty of often neglecting excitement, enjoyment and human flourishing in favour of gloom and doom analyses of the state of the world. One of the major purposes of sociology is to examine the social world for flaws and to challenge conservative claims that individuals can succeed and thrive if that is what they really want. However, there are limitations to understandings that fail to consider how people get by, even in fairly awful conditions, and sometimes even manage to enjoy themselves (Bennett 2011: 305). Acknowledging such enjoyment may be important but involve pitfalls. Whatever the place of optimism in intellectual terms, Oliver Bennett (2011) argues that the optimism of everyday life performs important social functions, especially in maintaining physical and psychological health, family and social relationships and in achieving goals. He suggests that these important functions are strongly supported by 'cultures of optimism' in which implicit cultural policies shore up optimistic outlooks, no matter how far from reality these may be. Yet he notes that it seems clear that these optimistic outlooks strengthen well-being. Optimism is linked to better health, even if just because optimists appear more likely to have healthy habits. In family life a certain degree of optimism is apparently essential to investing in the next generation and improving the quality of relationships. Achievement seems also to heavily rely on being optimistic, at least in as far as evidence suggests that being optimistic leads to working harder and is linked to better problem solving allied to a tendency to have a more comprehensive view of situations often successful in finding solutions to problems. It also seems evident that optimism is linked to electoral success, suggesting that positive visions of the future are found more compelling by the majority. Bennett (2011: 311–312) rightly admits that in examining optimism it should be noted that it is difficult to separate it from other elements of behaviour and that there are negative aspects to being optimistic as evident in the recent financial crisis. However, Bennett concludes that the institutionally supported implicit cultural policies (often in the form of governmental support for therapy) propping up optimism are needed because social pressures on family life have made it less able to fulfil this function. This is questionable. Some feminists have long argued that families never really were any good at providing a positive environment, or if they did, it would have been in ways that encouraged men to be optimistic, not women (for example Barrett and McIntosh 1982; Friedan 1965). Bennett's (2011) nuanced analysis of optimism may recognise the importance of people's hopes for better but he focuses too much on biology and he assumes that social organisation functions fairly well, which like most Functionalist approaches does not give enough attention to social inequalities or to conflict.

The expectations of a 'better' future implied in a sociology for optimists do not necessarily mean a future without inequality or conflict. For some, 'better' might mean happier, or at least more content. There are other versions where the focus might be on a future in which people are freer from oppression or social control. Yet, the pursuit of happiness may reinforce rather than lessen inequalities because the ability to pursue happiness is related to social structures (the way society is organised, for example around racial divisions), and how they determine the choices

individuals can and cannot make. Yet marginalised groups may provide alternative models for achieving happiness (Ahmed 2010). Human
enjoyment is not some sort of false consciousness, people are not simply
cultural dopes, slaves to consumerism or trying to escape the ever present
fear of risk. These are some of the different ways that sociologists have
accounted for the pleasure that people get from music or shopping or
other activities. All propose that people do not really enjoy these things
but only think they do because the media, other powerful groups or
common social ideas tell them they should. It is evident that sociologists are blind to certain aspects of everyday life (Kemple and Mawani
2009), but I contend that if sociology rejects optimistic ways of seeing,
its 'promise' (Back 2007; Mills 1959) is severely curtailed. Sociology's
implicit pessimism 'while it may give zest to the sociological enterprise,
limits the sociological imagination' (Killian 1971: 281; see also Flanagan
1976). Some optimism enhances the ability of sociologists to make sense
of the world and of how people make a way through it.[2] There is room
and need for a wider array of critical approaches that do not neglect the
negative but do acknowledge the positive.

One possible reason for the apparent lack of optimism within sociology is that it is often presented as a way of thinking that deals with
social problems, rather than just social questions (Groenemeyer 2007;
Mills 1943). In this sense, sociology could be seen as fundamentally based
on a 'disease model of human functioning' (Bennett 2011: 309). A social
problem is hard to define but can include all kinds of things that are seen
as negative aspects of social life such as crime, sexual violence, illness,
unemployment and poverty. These are some of the subjects of sociology and they indicate that sociology tends to draw attention to some
of the darker sides of human life. However, a pessimistic view is not
necessarily entailed in a focus on social problems. It is important to ask
questions about what is normal, who gets to define something as a problem, and should it therefore be eradicated (Killian 1971: 285; Mills 1943:
174–175)? For instance, it is important, but not apparently optimistic
to redefine sadness as a normal part of human experience rather than
always a sign of depression requiring medication (Horwitz and Wakefield
2007). To recognise sadness as part of the human experience refutes the
idea that sadness is a problem that needs fixing. Debilitating depression
must be acknowledged and treated, but in recommending better distinction between 'normal' sadness and clinical depression, Horwitz and
Wakefield are defending the diversity of human emotional experience
and can be interpreted as being critically optimistic about the benefits of
such diversity for people's well-being. Similarly, disappointment can be
articulated as crucial and to challenge its representation as negative can

provide a critically optimistic assessment of the major role that it plays in how people get by (Craib 1994). Looking at social problems can also be motivated by a desire for, and optimistic belief in, social change and thus provide a basis for finding solutions. It is very important to consider the flaws of current forms of social organisation if positive change is to occur. An account of optimistic threads within the history of sociology and their relation to more pessimistic ideas can help explain what a sociology for optimists might have to offer.

Breeding human beings more 'rationally' and basing a new religion on sociology were some of the now rather wacky seeming ideas of early sociologists, but they were based on optimistic ideas about progress. By looking back at the beginnings of sociology we can see that an optimistic stance was important in its development. Auguste Comte, the man who gave us the term 'sociology', came up with his ideas within the context of a scientific paradigm that was becoming centred around ideas of evolution and progress. However, many Victorian thinkers wrongly equated the two (Sklair 1970: 57–72). Having touched on Comte's account of the potential of sociology to comprehend the laws governing social life, the chapter then explores one version of sociological history. This covers the shift from Comte's hopes for sociology as a way of previsioning or imagining a 'better' world to Marx's revolutionary optimism. It continues by examining Weber's apparently pessimistic views of a disenchanted world and Durkheim's vision of social facts as revealing both hazards and hopefulness attached to the transition to modernity. A brief assessment is made of whether or not the twentieth century brought a pessimistic turn and why it might be important to reclaim critical forms of optimism.

Optimistic Origins?

August Comte's work, like that of many of his nineteenth century contemporaries could be classified as optimistic in terms of belief that progress is being made toward a better world. The concept of progress was not new and was evident within antiquity, but there emerged a new emphasis on the innovative kinds of progress arising from new ideas, processes or things (Sklair 1970: ix). For Comte science, and especially social science, was crucial in order to better understand the laws shaping social development. He tended, like many thinkers of the time, to assume that evolution, development and innovative progress all meant improvement (Sklair 1970: 64). He set out what he called a 'positive philosophy', although he did not mean an optimistic one, but an approach to knowledge that aims 'to discover, by a well-combined use of reasoning and observation, the actual laws of phenomena – that is to say, their invariable relations of succession and likeness' (Comte 1988: 2).

Unlike similar thinkers of the time (Bennett 2011: 302), Comte's optimism was not focused on the ability of human beings to shape their own world but on a now seemingly old-fashioned belief that there was a robust order to the social world. He believed that the social world was modified subject to natural laws which would bring an 'unquestionable' improvement to the condition and faculties of human beings. According to him, the speed of that progress, but not the order it took, could be altered. Comte believed that human attempts to modify the social world in his time were 'ill-regulated' because they were based on a poor understanding of how society works that ignored those natural laws. He thought that such attempts were also limited because they were political and thus part of the social and not above it. However, Comte argues that as sociology, the 'science of society', progresses it will reveal the natural laws and on that basis be able to 'prevision' or predict social phenomena (Comte 1858/1853). Just as natural sciences like physics understood the physical world by learning to understand the laws that governed it, he imagined sociology could set out the laws behind social behaviour. Later sociologists (Mills 1959) have questioned whether society does have any order or laws and whether just borrowing a method from the natural sciences is the best way to study it.

Comte is not only optimistic in seeing order to social life, but in believing that human beings can be better by living more rationally organised lives. Comte (1858/1853: 467) thinks happiness is too subjective a goal, depending on 'the entire system of circumstances' governing an individual's life and welfare and on the different social situations in which it variously arises. Thus, he argues that improvement means organising society on more 'scientific' principles and that means developing a better understanding of social life. For this to occur, Comte (1858/1853) saw it as first necessary to develop a means of investigation to elucidate both relations of order and processes of change. This method combined observation, directed and interpreted by theory, experiment, comparison and an historical method particularly important for the science of society. Social experiments were seen as possible if thought of in terms of interference with the regular course of a phenomenon, but this method was noted as less important. Instead he thought comparison of co-existing and past societies most important, whilst some comparison with other animals is also recommended[3] (see Chapter 8). This method demonstrated an optimistic orientation in its interesting emphasis on 'predicting' the past, or illuminating patterns of long-term social change as fundamental to sociological enterprise, something rather rarer in recent sociology (Inglis 2014). Arguably, Comte (1858/1853: 484) was also being optimistic in counselling sociologists to avoid thinking that a decrease of something will end in its extinction. Thus, Comte's ideas emerged at what is an optimistic moment, when notions of human progress towards more rationally organised and better lives were dominant.

Karl Marx was another apparently optimistic nineteenth century social thinker; his belief in progress focusing on movement towards greater freedom. Marx (1977/1864, 1983/1932) outlined the march of history as inexorably leading to the propertyless class overthrowing the capitalist system and its exploitative class relations. This he believed would result in communism, a system based on the collective power of individuals. Communism would bring a proper recognition of things and ideas as the products of human beings and their intercourse, so workers would have control over their work and their social contribution would be properly valued. Thus, although Marx analysed and criticised the appalling conditions under which workers laboured within the capitalist enterprises of his time, he saw this as a temporary phase. Marx thought capitalism would bring about its own end because of the contradiction it creates between the wealth and culture derived from its increase of productive power and its making of a mass of the population too poor to enjoy it. He argued that capitalism as a form of social structure determined the lives of individuals, and for most this meant barely surviving due to exploitation resulting in low wages and dirty and unhealthy working conditions:

> In short, by the introduction of machinery, the division of labour inside society has grown up, the task of the worker inside the workshop has been simplified, capital has been concentrated, human beings have been further dismembered. (Marx 1955/1847: 63)

However, Marx believed that it could and would be otherwise and that where 'philosophers have only interpreted the world, in various ways; the point is to change it' (Marx 1969/1888: VIII, XI). Thus he is a structural determinist, arguing that the material conditions and forms of social organisation under which people live and work are the most powerful shapers of their lives. Yet this is balanced against his belief in revolution and the coming of less exploitative ways of living and producing.

Whether the optimism of early sociology is related to beliefs in human progress towards more rational or to freer ways of living, it seems to trace to disappointing or disastrous outcomes. Comte's insistence on finding 'natural laws' underlying social life, and thus previsioning the future, link to a positivist version of sociology as science, perhaps most famously criticised by C. Wright Mills (1959) who instead argues that sociology is an imaginative enterprise. Mills (1943: 177) also points out that belief in progress is congenial to the academic men of the early twentieth century who were benefiting from the rising status of the middle classes.

Max Weber seems the arch representative of pessimism within sociology, as his vision of progress is of how it increasingly constrains human beings. However, there is optimistic potential in the 'defensive pessimism for the future of freedom [that] is a major theme of Weber's work' (Gerth and Mills 1970: 72). For Weber, history is a process of disenchantment, in which the magical and marvellous are ruthlessly banished by forces of rationalisation that see science and bureaucracy triumph but meaningfulness and individuality are lost. A sample of this pessimism appears in his 1918 prediction on the future of German politics. He warns that '[n]ot summer's bloom lies ahead of us, but rather a polar night of icy darkness, no matter what group may triumph externally now' and that only those who can 'brave even the crumbling of all hopes' have the calling for politics (Weber 1970/1948: 128). Yet even in that dark night he suggests that the crumbling of hopes can be braved, and other glimmers of optimism occasionally twinkle forth. Elsewhere he remarks that '[w]e cannot work without hoping that others will advance further than we have' (Weber 1970/1948: 136). This is hardly optimism at it brightest. However, while Weber diverges from ideas of his time that see progress towards a moral or technical betterment, there is some such idea inherent in what he says about increasing bureaucratisation, despite his belief that it would reduce the scope for exercising 'responsible freedom' (Gerth and Mills 1970: 51, 70). For instance, he notes that bureaucratisation is usually associated with 'the leveling of social differences', not least because it ends practices of appointing officials based on their privileged, often family, connections to the powerful. This does not inevitably result in the governed having more of a share of political power, but it is some sort of improvement (Weber 1970/1948: 225–244). Yet his overall pessimism about political and economic freedom is combined with 'pessimism about the realms of art, cultivation and the personality types possible for contemporary man' (Gerth and Mills 1970: 74). The latter is taken as a bequest by the Frankfurt School. If Weber is found to be pessimistic this might be explained by his personal psychological tendency toward depression, but that would not be very sociological. The social factors are obviously important, as he witnessed the rise and fall of his beloved German nation into and following the First World War. Yet France hardly offers a more hopeful homeland in the early twentieth century and yet the Frenchman Emile Durkheim is a more apparently optimistic member of the triumvirate (along with Marx and Weber) now routinely credited with founding sociology.

Durkheim's optimism is oriented towards belief in progress towards more freedom, but this freedom has a more individual and less political character than for Weber and Marx (Sklair 1970: 75). In *The Division of Labor in Society*, Durkheim (1933) argued that industrialisation, and the more complex specialised division of labour that it brought, had advantages in allowing for greater individuality. Prior to such industrialisation, societies tended to rely on mechanical solidarity, in which people were rather rigidly bonded together by their likeness. The kinds of lives that people led were very similar and they shared a common set of values. The similarities of people's lives and ways of thinking arose from the limited specialisation of functions within a more simple division of labour. Prior to industrialisation, the work of producing what is needed to survive was still relatively similar from one social group to another. Most people did a variety of things in a day; they may milk a cow in the morning, then bake bread, repair their house and spin or weave some wool. Individual rights were limited in the interests of maintaining social cohesion, because '[i]f we have a lively desire to think and act for ourselves, we cannot be strongly inclined to think and act as others do'. Under mechanical solidarity 'the individual does not appear' (Durkheim 1933: 130). In contrast, as the division of labour complexifies and greater specialisation of functions emerges, there is more room for individuality. This is because the kind of solidarity then produced is organic, as in more fluidly united, like 'the elements of an inanimate body' (Durkheim 1933: 130). Organic solidarity automatically arises from people's differences, differences now important because they are necessary to the different tasks they must perform. As Durkheim (1933: 131) says, 'on the one hand, each one depends as much more strictly on society as labor is more divided; and on the other, the activity of each is as much more personal as it is more specialized'. For example, if someone is busy all day making cotton textiles in a factory, they need to rely on others to bake bread for them to eat, or build houses for them. There are still limitations on individuals but 'the yoke that we submit to is much less heavy than when society completely controls us' (Durkheim 1933: 131). Nevertheless, Durkheim's seeming optimism about the improvements brought by organic solidarity are tempered by his awareness that social change does not integrate everyone equally into society and that both over-integration and under-integration can produce a state of anomie, where social norms may be unclear and confused and individuals disconnected from others. Pessimism is not absent.

There is a subjective element to labelling particular 'founders' as optimistic or pessimistic, and there are other stories to be told of how sociology developed and who are the important thinkers. Connell (2007) argues that claiming Marx, Weber and Durkheim as the founding fathers is fairly recent, a late twentieth century version of sociological history. She notes the Eurocentric nature of such versions and others point out the way in which they ignore women thinkers such as Harriet Martineau or Jane Addams (Deegan 2013; Delamont 1992; Hill and Hoecker-Drysdale 2001). And why focus on big names rather than the more grassroots practice of sociology? There are optimistic threads to tease out from more routine histories of doing sociology. Here the UK is discussed, leaving the optimism of other national contexts for another time.

Making a Better World?

The optimism of early twentieth century British sociologists lay in seeing sociology 'as a means of making possible effective social action' (Halliday 1968: 378). For example, within Britain a Sociological Society was established in 1904, to 'promote the study of sociology at university'. It has been argued that the three types of sociology prominent in the UK at the time can be discerned within the society: eugenics, civic sociology and ethical sociology (Halliday 1968). For my purposes, what is most interesting about this 'lost' history of sociology (Renwick 2011, 2012) is that each of the three versions of sociology has what can be described as an optimistic bent. Some, however, had less than happy or free consequences. Historians of sociology may vary slightly on what happened to these different kinds of sociology, but agree that it was the ethical school that triumphed in the end, with one of its main proponents, Hobhouse becoming the first Professor of Sociology in the UK (Halliday 1968; Halsey 2004; Renwick 2011, 2012). I want to consider what the implications were for optimism within sociology.

Eugenics was certainly optimistic but is probably an aspect of sociology's past most would like to forget. Eugenicists saw uncontrolled breeding as the major social problem and sought to educate or legislate for more 'rational' reproduction. This meant encouraging influences that enhance 'inborn' qualities and those that 'develop them to the utmost advantage' (Galton, cited in Renwick 2011: 366). Eugenics is now seen as dubious because of its association with Fascism and the holocaust, bur prior to that the idea of breeding 'better' human beings was very popular. The close association of eugenics with the emergence of sociology in Britain is evident in Francis Galton, who coined the term eugenics, choosing a 1904 meeting of the Sociological Society as a platform to launch his ideas for a national campaign of eugenics. However, Galton did not believe in creating supermen, because he understood that variation is essential in evolution. He thought all humans could be improved through educating people. The aim was to make people aware of how reproduction worked so that they could make choices which would result in a better world. These ideas were situated within the context of late nineteenth and early twentieth century concerns over the poor physical conditions of men volunteering to fight for their country and the poor health such classes suffered due to their living and working conditions. Class prejudices also shaped worries that the higher birth rate of the working classes compared to the middle classes would lead to degeneration of the species. Yet how the actual biological laws of inheritance worked was poorly understood and thus Galton himself relied on statistical analysis of those who were socially successful to try to prove that traits were inherited. He exhorted sociologists to provide similar data, for instance on those who had achieved upward social mobility. Thus eugenics, in this early form, was a project for social reform (Halliday 1968; Renwick 2011). It involved being optimistic about how social science understandings could produce healthier and more capable human beings. Nazi adaptation of eugenic principles in the service of bigotry and mass extermination of Jews, homosexuals and other minority groups, snapped this optimistic thread under the weight of so much blood that any effort to reclaim it seems not only doomed but offensive. We must look elsewhere.

Civic and ethical forms of sociology seem more promising places to learn about sociological forms of optimism aimed at actively changing society for the better, and they have their counterparts outside of Britain. The ethical sociologists focused on training social workers to help in solving social problems through charitable work, while the civic sociologists thought urban planning – altering the environment – was the way to improve individual and social life (Halliday 1968). In Britain, civic sociology had its centre in Edinburgh (Halliday 1968). The American version had its most famous incarnation in the Chicago School of the late nineteenth and early twentieth century. Initially it included sociologists who were oriented to using social work to improve the lives of ordinary people. The latter, however, were largely women centred around Jane Addams and Hull House and they later split, or were forced off into other subject areas such as social work or home economics. Their contribution to sociology was under-valued or even ignored by the later largely male 'Chicago School' sociologists, like Robert Parks (Deegan 2013; Delamont 1992). In Britain, it was Hobhouse's inauguration as the first British Professor of Sociology that shifted emphasis away from town planning (which he rejected) and towards ethical sociology and its emphasis on human reason as the driving force of social development. For Hobhouse, '[s]ocial life was made by rational initiatives for ends ethically justifiable' (Halliday 1968: 388). Although the three threads of British sociology were initially brought together in the Sociological Society, Hobhouse had the institutional backing of the University of London and was the only chair of sociology. He was also editor of the Society's journal *The Sociological Review*, (which superseded the *Papers of the Sociology Society*). His own hostility to eugenics and to civics drove those social scientists off to form their own organisations. Meanwhile, sociology became oriented towards practical application via social work intended to instil cooperative ideals in the population (Halliday 1968). The problem with this sociological optimism was that it became entangled with sometimes dubious forms of social engineering (Killian 1971: 286), in which the state co-opts social science ideas and uses them in efforts to better control and subdue populations (Foucault 1992; cf. Mills 1959).

A Sociology for Optimists in a New World

During the early years of the twentieth century, optimism declined in sociology (Sklair 1970: 73–88), although it did not completely disappear. The ability of (social) science to predict and assist in speeding up human progress was seriously called into question, after two world wars in which science was mostly used to mass produce death. For instance, scientists created atom bombs capable of destroying the human race and facilitated mass human killing in the Nazi's 'final solution' (Adorno and Horkheimer 1979/1944; Bauman 1989). The Frankfurt School that emerged as a sociological force in the middle of the twentieth century understandably contained considerable pessimism given that many were German Jews who had fled to escape the holocaust, and were faced with the historical horrors of Fascism and Stalinism. Their intellectual context arguably also fed this pessimism, because they were unable to overcome the limits of traditional Marxism given that they did not fundamentally reconstitute its dialectical critique. A dialectic tries to establish the truth via an exchange of reasoned arguments. The Frankfurt School only slightly adapted Marxism. Instead of labour being the basis for critical thought and for emancipation, production was seen as developing towards domination

(Postone and Brick 1982). For others, the pessimism of the school can be seen as centred on their critique of instrumental rationality (Bennett 2011: 302), but there is room to debate the triumph of reason over emotions, and indeed a need to be critical of assumptions that they are mutually exclusive. Emotion informs our reasoning and reasoning can produce emotions (Holmes 2010). However, the Frankfurt School's critical theory was also hopeful, it contained robust thinking about how the world might be otherwise – including 'better'.

More problematic was the dispositional form of optimism evident in the Functionalist sociology so dominant in America from the 1940s to 1960s. The key figure was Talcott Parsons (Killian 1971: 281). In so far as Talcott Parsons can be said to have had an optimistic disposition, this may have been a product of the social reform values instilled in him as the son of a Protestant minister in Colorado, and of his studying under the ethical sociologists at the London School of Economics. Yet this is mixed with his close association with Weberian thought via his time in Heidelberg, resulting in him being responsible for translating many of Weber's works into English (Robertson and Turner 1989: 540–541). In his bringing of European social theory into American sociology, his work contrasts with:

> much of American sociology [which] was guided by the optimistic view that the research findings of applied sociology could directly inform the political process to bring about a reform of the urban environment. (Robertson and Turner 1989: 541)

Parsons's close attachment to the primarily pessimistic worldview of Weber, perhaps evident in his pessimism about human mortality (Gouldner 1970: 433), was somewhat ameliorated by his later turning to Durkheim (1933: 405). However, his optimistic disposition can help account for his flawed analysis of the importance of shared values in maintaining social order. He shares with Durkheim the attempt to understand how achieving 'the ideal of human fraternity' might be linked to the increasing complexification of modern societies. Parsons also shares with Durkheim an interest in how social order is achieved through integration. For Parsons (1989: 581) this means recognising 'the existence and importance of a single unified value system' that he believes remains largely stable over time. In examining the American value system he sees its instrumental orientation on getting things done as in contrast to both utopian and 'end-of-the-world-is-nigh' value systems (Parsons 1989: 595). Yet while he may evaluate American values as neither overly optimistic nor pessimistic, he is optimistic in his own thinking that the capitalist system can be gradually reformed to integrate all people more happily. For Parsons the world is the 'best possible of worlds, ever growing better' (Gouldner 1970: 432). One indication of his too sanguine views on capitalism is his claim that 'the extremely high valuation of the executive role within our occupational system' is based primarily on the valuing of 'worthwhile' collective performances that he believes are facilitated by those who create and operate organisations (Parsons 1989: 599). This lacks critical consideration of the coopera-tion of workers as achieving 'worthwhile' outcomes, which may in fact be hindered rather than helped by management decrees and policies (Burawoy 1979). Overall, much of Parsons's work (for example, Parsons 1951; Parsons and Shils 2001/1951) tends to be overly optimistic about the importance of humans normatively choosing goals and yet overly pessimistic about the way in which the functioning of the social sys-tem structures human relations (cf. Robertson and Turner 1989: 544). However, it is his supposed optimism that is at the foundation of many criticisms of him, and for all his faults it is worth considering this further.

There are elements of Parsons's work which show a more strate-gic employment of optimism to criticise ideas about how people act within social constraints. For example, there is optimism in Parsons's sus-tained criticism of rational choice models of social and economic action (Robertson and Turner 1989: 548). His acknowledgement of normative but non-rational constraints on people combines (albeit uneasily) with a view of human beings as exercising agency (Parsons 1937). His optimism can be read not just in a static view of social stability but in 'a broader concern with the historical and comparative conditions for political change within an environment which would permit the development of individual freedoms and collective stability' (Robertson and Turner 1989: 548). This is not to deny the pitfalls of his bad writing and overly complex abstraction of ideas into 'Grand Theory' (Mills 1959: 25–49), but it is perhaps the kind of optimism that Parsons offers which is at fault: his dispositional optimism. It is, according to Gouldner (1970: 434):

> an optimism in the face of pessimism, an optimism that rejects and is against pessimism. Optimism need not be of that sort. It can simply be born of the prospects, excitement and enjoy-ment of life; it can express a sense of the juices that run through one ... [his optimism in being so determined is] so little able to acknowledge any serious difficulty in our society or to see any of its problems in their full profundity.

Such criticism coincided with the waning of Parsons's always debated star as his supposed lack of a theory of power or conflict seemed increasingly problematic within the rise to dominance of conflict theories of sociology from the 1970s onwards (see Gouldner 1970).

Also crucial to a sociology for optimists are the more global sociologies that can provide understanding of our new world. This requires understanding of modernity in both new world and old as founded not just on the exploitation of the working classes, but on the oppression of women and the enslavement or conquering of black peoples and colonisation of their lands (Bhambra 2007; Connell 2007; McLennan 2003). A focus on postcoloniality is partly prompted by my own positionality as a white scholar born in Aotearoa/New Zealand, a former British colony. Yet this is not just an attempt to make sense of my own personal biography in relation to wider history (Mills 1959) but to see how non-European and non-American thinkers might prompt different kinds of critically optimistic sociological thinking based on different histories.

As the millennium approached, scholars based in Europe or America advanced critiques of colonisation and slavery that were optimistic in their hopes to reveal and shift inequalities. Non-white scholars living and working largely outside Europe and America have been less well recognised (Connell 2007). Mostly non-white writers, from sociology and allied disciplines, have highlighted the need to understand colonisation and the past experiences of the colonised and enslaved in order to analyse and address contemporary inequalities around race (see, for example, Davis 1981; Hall 1996; Hill-Collins 1990; Spivak 1988). Colonisation was strongly connected to capitalist expansion, as wealthy nations plundered the natural and human resources of the 'new world'. Slave plantations were established in the Americas and Caribbean, Africa and India were mined and farmed. New territories also offered new ways to deal with the social problems of Europe (Woollacott, 2006), such as a shortage of land, overcrowded cities and crime. Australia, for instance, became a British penal colony. Beliefs in white superiority also played a part in justifying European invasion of countries far from their shores. By reminding Europeans of their past, these academics provided a history in which biographies of both white and non-white peoples could be understood as part of a wider history. Thus aspects of racial inequality that may seem like personal troubles could potentially begin to be understood as public issues (Bhambra 2007; Mills 1959). In America, there was important feminist work on black identities, the representation of black women and the difficulties this raised for the feminist movement. Many of the key works involved efforts to consider how black and/or postcolonial subjects might overcome their voiceless invisibility or misrepresentation (for example, Davis 1981; hooks 1992; Spivak 1988).

The optimism of many critics of colonialism has often been directed toward revolutionary change. One of the most influential in the later twentieth century being Franz Fanon (1968/1961). His argument is that colonised peoples are oppressed by the lack of recognition of colonisers as well as by force. He highlights historical portrayals of black people as animals, or at best as 'noble savages'. This lack of recognition leads the colonised to envy the colonisers and mimic them. Yet they are never accepted and always othered, which produces psychic wretchedness to add to their material deprivation. However, he argues that through violence of their own the oppressed can achieve catharsis and gain political and personal independence. This form of critical optimism may feel sociologically uncomfortable, situated as it is within a psychoanalytic perspective and relying on bloody armed struggle for overcoming oppression. The psychoanalytic focus may individualise the effects of colonisation in ways problematic to most sociologists, and pacifists like myself may wish to take issue with whether more violence is likely to provide a solution to past injustice. However, discomfort can move people and ideas and Fanon's work is important also because it proposes that it is possible for the colonised to break free of Westernised thinking; that it is possible for peoples who have been subjected via imperialist thought and actions to think for themselves and to think themselves. In this light Linda Tuhiwai Smith's (1999) book on *Decolonising Methodologies* is just one example, albeit again influential, of a thoroughgoing criticism of the way that Western research has taken indigenous ideas and artefacts for its own purposes. It is also critically optimistic in the way that it centres and makes real the possibility of indigenous people's not just taking back but taking control of that knowledge and making their world their own. The challenge for white Western scholars is to learn from these different ways of thinking without appropriating them again. I have endeavoured to give some examples within the book of how this might be possible, partly by thinking with and around different concepts and issues such as connection to nature, land and some kind of spiritual meaning (Tuhiwai-Smith 1999). In order to do so the forms of critical thinking needed are ones which can contribute to possibilities for positive change, rather than celebrating social order.

Conclusion

Although this is a very imprecise and partial overview of sociology, it gives some indication of the different forms of optimistic orientations in sociology and some possible histories. These histories help illustrate the necessity of some degree of optimism in doing sociology, but also some of the pitfalls involved. The point is to learn from this history how to include an optimistic stance as part of thinking sociologically. Optimism is not simply cruel (Berlant 2011). Early sociologists were optimistic about progress towards a 'better' world, whether they imagined what might be better in terms of a more rationally ordered society or greater collective or individual freedom. As well as these wider theoretical developments, as sociology took particular shape in specific places, there were debates about how it could be used to actually bring about a better world. I have given one account of these debates in the UK, where the dawn of the twentieth century saw budding sociologists argue for eugenics or urban planning or ethically based forms of social work as best for improving social life. The ethical school became prominent, largely because it had the institutional backing of the UK's first Professor of Sociology, Leonard Hobhouse. However, the connection to social work was later weakened by the development of a separate social work discipline and other versions of sociology gradually emerged. What this brief sketch of some of the history of sociology can tell us is that there is a strong optimistic thread within sociological thinking and it is worth rethinking its benefits. Pessimism alone cannot provide a full understanding of the complexity of the social world and optimism is a crucial tool for sociologists. An optimistic approach takes effort, it does not only see harmony, but can explore the conflict and struggles involved in creating change for the better, or seeking greater freedom. An optimistic sociology can make us think about how to live a good life, how to make a more equal society and how to maintain nourishing relationships with others. It can even foster hopes and plans for averting the destruction of our planet. All sociologists need to be optimists – at least sometimes.

Notes

1. For evidence of the latter see Saskia Sassen's recent work, for example Sassen (2014).
2. I borrow this terminology of 'making our way through the world' from Margaret Archer (2003, 2007) who uses it to describe how reflexivity mediates between structure and agency.
3. The latter was more controversial in Comte's time, when human beings were seen in Christian terms as at the apex of a hierarchy of God's creations and comparing them to animals as somewhat sacrilegious. This was also a major aspect of the furore surrounding Darwin's theory of evolution.

REFERENCES

Abend, G. (2008) 'Two main problems in the sociology of morality', *Theory and Society*, 37(2): 87–125.

Abbott, P., Wallace, C. and Sapsford, R. (2011) 'Surviving the transformation: social quality in Central Asia and the Caucuses', *Journal of Happiness Studies*, 12(2): 199–223.

Adorno, T. and Horkheimer, M. (1979/1944) *Dialectic of Enlightenment*. London: Verso.

Ahmed, S. (2004) 'Affective economies', *Social Text*, 22(2): 117–139.

Ahmed, S. (2010) *The Promise of Happiness*. Durham, NC: Duke University Press.

Albrow, M. (1990) *Max Weber's Construction of Social Theory*. London: Macmillan.

Archer, M. S. (1993) 'Bourdieu's theory of cultural reproduction: French or universal?', *French Cultural Studies*, 4: 225–240.

Archer, M. S. (2003) *Structure, Agency and the Internal Conversation*. Cambridge: Cambridge University Press.

Archer, M.S. (2007) *Making Our Way Through the World: Human Reflexivity and Social Mobility*. Cambridge: Cambridge University Press.

Archer, M.S. (2010) 'Routine, reflexivity and realism', *Sociological Theory*, 28(3): 272–303.

Attwood, B. and Markus, A. (1999) *The Struggle for Aboriginal Rights: A Documentary History*. Sydney: Allen and Unwin.

Aud, S., Fox, M. and Kewal Ramani, A. (2010) 'Status and Trends in the Education of Racial and Ethnic Groups. NCES 2010–2015', *National Center for Education Statistics*, available at: http://eric.ed.gov/?id=ED510909 (accessed 17 November 2014).

Australian Bureau of Statistics (2014) 'Indigenous Status of Prisoners'. 4517.0 – Prisoners in Australia, 2013, available at: www.abs.gov.au/ausstats/abs@.nsf/Lookup/by%20Subject/4517.0~2013~Main%20Features~Indigenous%20status%20of%20prisoners~13 (accessed 21 November 2014).

Badiou, A. (2001) *Ethics: An Essay on the Understanding of Evil*. London and New York: Verso.

Badiou, A. (2007) *De Quoi Sarkozy est-il le Nom?* Paris: Nouvelles Éditions Lignes.

Back, L. (2007) *The Art of Listening*. Oxford and New York: Berg.

Bailey, J. (1988) *Pessimism*. London: Routledge

Bailey, J. (2003) *Unquiet Lives: Marriage and Marriage Breakdown in England, 1660–1800*. Cambridge: Cambridge University Press.

Bakker, E. and de Leede, S. (2015) 'European Female Jihadists in Syria: Exploring an Under-Researched Topic'. ICCT background note. Hague: International Centre for Counter-Terrorism. Available at: www.icct.nl/download/file/ICCT-Bakker-de-Leede-European-Female-Jihadists-In-Syria-Exploring-An-Under-Researched-Topic-April2015.pdf (accessed 5 May 2015).

Baldassar, L., Baldock, C. and Wilding, R. (2007) *Families Caring Across Borders: Migration, Ageing and Transnational Caregiving*. Basingstoke: Palgrave Macmillan.

Bancroft, A., Zimpfer, M. J., Murray, O. and Karels, M. (2014) 'Working at pleasure in young women's alcohol consumption: a participatory visual ethnography', *Sociological Research Online*, 19(3). 10.5153/sro.3409.

Barker, N. (2012) *Not the Marrying Kind: A Feminist Critique of Same-Sex Marriage*. Basingstoke: Palgrave Macmillan.

Barrett, M. and McIntosh, M. (1982) *The Anti-Social Family*. London: NLB.

Barro, R.J and Lee, J.W. (2013) 'A new dataset of educational attainment in the world, 1950–2010', *Journal of Development Economics*, 104: 184–198.

Bartkowski, J. P. (2004) *The Promise Keepers: Servants, Soldiers and Godly Men*. New Brunswick, NJ: Rutgers University Press.

Bauman, Z. (1976) *Socialism: The Active Utopia*. London: Allen and Unwin.

Bauman, Z. (1989) *Modernity and the Holocaust*. Ithaca, NY: Cornell University Press.

Bauman, Z. (1995) *Life in Fragments: Essays in Postmodern Morality*. Oxford: Blackwell.

Bauman, Z. (2008) *Does Ethics Have a Chance in a World of Consumers?* Cambridge, MA: Harvard University Press.

Baxter, J. (2013) 'Gender, justice and domestic work: life course transitions and perceptions of fairness', *Longitudinal and Lifecourse Studies*, 4(1): 78–85.

BBC (2014) 'Where is it Illegal to be Gay?', available at: www.bbc.co.uk/world-25927595.

Beasley, C. and Bacchi, C. (2012) 'Making politics fleshly', in A. Bletsas and C. Beasley (eds) *Engaging with Carol Bacchi: Strategic Interventions and Exchanges*. Adelaide: University of Adelaide Press, pp. 99–120.

Beasley, C., Brook, H. and Holmes, M. (2012) *Heterosexuality in Theory and Practice*. London: Routledge.

Beck, U. (2007) 'Beyond class and nation: reframing social inequalities in a globalizing world', *British Journal of Sociology*, 58(4): 679–705.

Beck, U. and Beck-Gernsheim, E. (1995) *The Normal Chaos of Love*. Cambridge: Polity Press.

Beck, U. and Beck-Gernsheim, E. (2002) *Individualization: Institutionalized Individualism and its Social and Political Consequences*. London: Sage.

Becker, H.S. (1967) 'Whose side are we on?', *Social Problems*, 14(3): 239–247.

Beer, D. (2008) 'Making friends with Jarvis Cocker: music culture in the context of web 2.0', *Cultural Sociology*, 2(2): 222–241.

Benavot, A. and Riddle, P. (1988) 'The expansion of primary education, 1870–1940: trends and issues', *Sociology of Education*, 61(3): 191–210.

Benhabib, S. (1987) 'The generalized and the concrete other: The Kohlberg-Gilligan controversy and Feminist Theory', in S. Benhabib and D. Cornell (eds) *Feminism as Critique*. Minneapolis, MN: University of Minnesota Press, pp. 77–95.

Bennett, O. (2011) 'Cultures of optimism', *Cultural Sociology,* 5(2): 301–320.

Bentley, P.J., Coates, H., Dobson, I.R., Goedegebuure, L., and Meek, V.L. (2013) *Job Satisfaction Around the Academic World*. New York and London: Springer.

Berlant, L. (2011) *Cruel Optimism*. Durham, NC and London: Duke University Press.

Betterton, R. (1987) *Looking On: Images of Femininity in the Visual Arts and Media*. London: Routledge.

Bhambra, G.K. (2007) *Rethinking Modernity: Postcolonialism and the Sociological Imagination*. Basingstoke: Palgrave Macmillan.

Billett, P. (2014) 'Dark cloud or silver lining? the value of bonding networks during youth', *Journal of Youth Studies* 17(7): 847–856.

Bishop, E.C. and Willis, K. (2014) '"Without hope everything would be gloom and doom": young people talk about the importance of hope in their lives', *Journal of Youth Studies* online, 17(6): 778–793.

Black, P. (2004) *The Beauty Industry: Gender, Culture, Pleasure*. London and New York: Routledge.

Black, R., Adger, W.N., Arnell, N.W., Dercon, S., Geddes, A. and Thomas, D. (2011) 'The effect of environmental change on human migration', *Global Environmental Change,* 21: S3–S11.

Bleich, E. (2014) 'Freedom of Expression versus Racist Hate Speech: Explaining Differences Between High Court Regulations in the USA and Europe', *Journal of Ethnic and Migration Studies,* 40(2): 283–300.

Blumstein, A. (2015) 'Racial disproportionality in prison', in R. Bangs and L.E. Davis (eds) *Race and Social Problems: Restructuring Inequality.* New York: Springer, pp. 187–194.

Bohrnstedt, G., Kitmitto, S., Ogut, B., Sherman, D., and Chan, D. (2015) School Composition and the Black–White Achievement Gap (NCES 2015-018). U.S. Department of Education, Washington, DC: National Center for Education Statistics. Accessed 26 January, 2016 at http://nces.ed.gov/pubsearch.

Bolhuis, J.J., Brown, G.R., Richardson, R.C. and Laland, K.N. (2011) 'Darwin in mind: new opportunities for evolutionary psychology', *PLoS Biology,* 9(7): e1001109.

Boliver, V. (2011) 'Expansion, differentiation, and the persistence of social class inequalities in British higher education', *Higher Education,* 61(3): 229–242.

Bongaarts, J. (2006) 'Late marriage and the HIV epidemic in sub-Saharan Africa', *Population Studies* 61(1): 73–83.

Booth, M. (1990) *The Triads: The Chinese Criminal Fraternity.* London: Grafton Books.

Bourdieu, P. (1987) *Distinction: A Social Critique of the Judgement of Taste.* Cambridge, MA: Harvard University Press.

Bourdieu, P. and Passeron, J. (1977) *Reproduction in Education, Society and Culture.* London: Sage.

Braverman, H. (1975) *Labor and Monopoly Capital: The Degradation of Work in the Twentieth Century.* New York and London: Monthly Review Press.

Bridges, L. (2012) 'Four days in August: The UK Riots', *Race & Class,* 54(1): 1–12.

Bringle, R. and Buunk, B. (1991) 'Jealousy and extra-dyadic relationships', in K. McKinney and S. Sprecher (eds) *Sexuality in Close Relationships.* Hillsdale, NJ: Erlbaum, pp. 135–153.

Brownlie, J. (2014) *Ordinary Relationships: A Sociological Study of Emotions, Reflexivity and Culture.* Basingstoke: Palgrave Macmillan.

Brownmiller, S. (1975) *Against Our Will: Men, Women and Rape.* London: Secker and Warburg.

Bruce, S. (2002) *God is Dead: Secularization in the West.* Oxford: Blackwell.

Bryant, C.D. (1979) 'The zoological connection: animal-related human behavior', *Social Forces,* 58(2): 399–421.

Bryman, A. (2004) *The Disneyization of Society.* London: Sage.

Buchanan, A.E. (1987) 'Marx, morality, and history: an assessment of recent analytical work on Marx', *Ethics,* 98(1): 104–136.

Bulbeck, C. (2009) *Sex, Love and Feminism in the Asia Pacific: A Cross-cultural Study of Young People's Attitudes.* Oxford and New York: Routledge.

Bumpass, L. and Lu, H.H. (2000) 'Trends in cohabitation and implications for children's family contexts in the United States', *Population Studies,* 54(1): 29–41.

Burawoy, M. (1979) *Manufacturing Consent: Changes in the Labor Process Under Monopoly Capitalism.* Chicago, IL and London: University of Chicago Press.

Burawoy, M. (2005) '2004 presidential address: Michael Burawoy, For public sociology', *American Sociological Review,* 70(1): 4–28.

Burkitt, I. (2005), 'Powerful emotions: power, government and opposition in the "war on terror"', *Sociology,* 39(4): 679–95.

Burkitt, I. (2012) 'Emotional reflexivity: feeling, emotion and imagination in reflexive dialogues', *Sociology,* 46(3): 458–72.

Buttel, F.H., Dickens, P., Dunlap, R.E. and Gijswijt, A. (2002) 'Sociological theory and the environment, an overview', in R.H. Dunlap, F.H. Buttel, P. Dickens and A. Gijswijt (eds) *Sociological Theory and the Environment: Classical Foundations, Contemporary Insights.* Lanham, MD: Rowman and Littlefield, pp. 3–29.

Camacho, G.B. (2008) 'Economic well-being among elderly couples in marriage and cohabitation in Mexico', *Población y Salud en Mesoamérica,* 6(1): 1–29.

Campbell, C. (1987) *The Romantic Ethic and the Spirit of Modern Consumerism.* Oxford: Blackwell.

Carroll, W.K. (2009) 'Transnationalists and national networkers in the global corporate elite', *Global Networks,* 9(3): 289–314.

Castells, M. (2012) *Networks of Outrage and Hope: Social Movements in the Internet Age.* Cambridge: Polity Press.

Castoriadis, C. (1987) *The Imaginary Institution of Society*. Cambridge: Polity Press.

CCCS Women's Group (1978) *Women Take Issue*. London: Hutchinson.

Central Intelligence Agency (2014) 'Country Comparison: GDP (purchasing power parity)', in *The World Factbook*, available at: https://www.cia.gov/library/publications/the-world-factbook/rankorder/2001rank.html (accessed 23 October 2014).

Chamblis, W.J. (1989) 'STATE-ORGANIZED CRIME—The American Society of Criminology, 1988 Presidential Address', *Criminology*, 27(2): 183–208.

Chan, K-B (2014) 'Entertainment: enjoyment or struggle?', in Chan, K-B (ed.) *Chinese Entertainment*. Abingdon and New York: Routledge, pp. 1–6.

Chan, K-B and Yung, S-S (2014) 'Chinese entertainment, ethnicity and pleasure', in Chan, K-B (ed.) *Chinese Entertainment*. Abingdon and New York: Routledge, pp. 7–46.

Charles, M. (2011) 'A world of difference: international trends in women's economic status', *Annual Review of Sociology,* 37: 355–371.

China Post (2010) 'Newlywed's divorce rates soar in China', 26 January, available at: www.chinapost.com.tw/china/national-news/2010/01/26/242331/Newlyweds-divorce.htm (accessed 29 April 2011).

Chowdhury, S. (2011) 'Employment in India: what does the latest data show?', *Economic and Political Weekly,* XLVI(32): 23–6.

Chu, Y. K. (2000) *The Triads as Business*. London: Routledge.

Clark, N. (2011) 'After the tsunami: vulnerability on a volatile planet', in *Inhuman Nature: Social Life on a Dynamic Planet*. London: Sage, pp 55–80.

Cohen, S. and Taylor, L. (1992) *Escape Attempts: The Theory and Practice of Resistance in Everyday Life*. London Routledge.

Comte, A. (1858/1853) 'Characteristics of the positive method in its application to social phenomena' in *The Positive Philosophy of Auguste Comte*. Transl. by Harriet Martineau. New York: Calvin Blanchard, pp. 452–485.

Comte, A. (1988) *Introduction to Positive Philosophy,* translated by F. Ferré (ed). Indianapolis, IN: Hackett Publishing.

Connell, R. (2007) *Southern Theory*. Cambridge: Polity Press.

Connell, R. (2011) *Confronting Equality: Gender, Knowledge and Global Change*. Cambridge: Polity Press.

Connell, R. W., Ashenden, D., Kessler, S. and Dowsett, G. (1982) *Making the Difference: Schools, Families and Social Division*. Sydney: Allen & Unwin.

Cook, A. and Glass, C. (2014) 'Above the glass ceiling: when are women and racial/ethnic minorities promoted to CEO?', *Strategic Management Journal,* 35: 1080–1089.

Cortis, N. and Newmarch, E. (2000) *Boys in Schools: What's Happening?*. Canberra: Equity Section, Analysis and Equity Branch, Department of Education, Training and Youth Affairs.

Craib, I. (1994) *The Importance of Disappointment*. London: Routledge.

Crenshaw, K. (1989) 'Demarginalizing the intersection of race and sex: a black feminist critique of antidiscrimination doctrine, feminist theory and anti-racist politics', *The University of Chicago Legal Forum*, 139–67.

Crouch, C. (2004) *Post-Democracy*. Cambridge: Polity Press.

Csikszentmihalyi, M. (1997) *Finding Flow: The Psychology of Engagement with Everyday Life*. New York: HarperCollins.

Damasio, A. (2000) *The Feeling of What Happens: Body and Emotion in the Making of Consciousness.* New York: Harcourt.

Davidson, M.J. and Burke, R.J. (2011) 'Women in management worldwide: Progress and prospects – An overview', in M.J. Davidson and R.J. Burke (eds) *Women in Management Worldwide: Progress and Prospects*. Farnham: Gower, pp 1–20.

Davie, G. (2001) 'The persistence of institutional religion in modern Europe', in L. Woodhead, P. Heelas and D. Martin (eds) *Peter Berger and the Study of Religion*. London: Routledge, pp. 101–111.

Davie, G. (2013) 'Preface to the Second Edition', in *The Sociology of Religion: A Critical Agenda*. London: Sage, pp. xi–xx.

Davis, A.Y. (1981) *Women, Race and Class*. London: Women's Press.

Dawkins, R. (1989[1976]) *The Selfish Gene*. Oxford: Oxford University Press.

Deegan, M.J. (2013) 'Jane Addams, the Hull-House school of sociology, and social justice, 1892 to 1935', *Humanity & Society*, 37(3): 248–258.

Delamont, S. (1992) 'Old fogies and intellectual women: an episode in academic history', *Women's History Review*, 1(1): 39–61.

Delhey, J. and Kohler, U. (2012) 'Happiness inequality. adding meaning to numbers – a reply to Veenhoven and Kalmijn', *Social Science Research*, 41: 731–734.

Delphy, C. (1984) *Close to Home: A Materialist Analysis of Women's Oppression*. London: Hutchinson.

Department for Culture, Media and Sport (2014) 'Secondary Analysis of the Gender Pay Gap' March, available at: www.equalpayportal.co.uk/statistics/ (accessed 5 November 2014).

Department of Education (2014) 'Statistical Release A level and other Level 3 Results (Provisional): 2013/14, 23 October', available at: https://www.gov.uk/government/uploads/system/uploads/attachment_data/file/365986/SFR42_2014_provisional__A_level_and_level_3_SFR.pdf (accessed 6 November 2014).

De Vaus, D. and Richardson, S. (2009) 'Living alone in Australia: trends in sole living and characteristics of those who live alone', Occasional Paper 2009: Census Series Number 4, Academy of the Social Sciences in Australia, available at: http://www.assa.edu.au/publications/occasional_papers/2009_CS4.php (accessed 18 July 2012).

Devereux, S. (2001) 'Sen's entitlement approach: critiques and counter-critiques', *Oxford Development Studies*, 29(3): 245–263.

Dines, G. and Humez, J.M. (eds) (2011) *Gender, Race and Class in Media: A Critical Reader*. London and Thousand Oaks, CA: Sage.

Domínguez-Folgueras, M. (2013) 'Is cohabitation more egalitarian? the division of household labor in five European countries', *Journal of Family Issues*, 34(12): 1623–1646.

Doty, A. (1993) *Making Things Perfectly Queer: Interpreting Mass Culture.* Minneapolis, MN: University of Minnesota Press.

Duffy, R. (2002) *A Trip Too Far: Ecotourism, Politics, and Exploitation.* London: Earthscan.

Duncan, S., Edwards, R., Reynolds, T. and Alldred, P. (2003) 'Motherhood, paid work and partnering: values and theories', *Work, Employment and Society,* 17(2): 309–330.

Durkheim, E. (1933/1964) *The Division of Labor in Society.* Glencoe, IL: Free Press.

Durkheim, E. (1938) *The Rules of Sociological Method* (SA Solovay & JH Mueller, Trans.), (GEG Catlin ed.). Glencoe, IL: The Free Press. (Original work published 1895).

Easterlin, R.A. (2001) 'Income and happiness: towards a unified theory', *The Economic Journal,* 111: 465–484.

Ehrenreich, B. (2007) *Dancing in the Streets: A History of Collective Joy.* London: Granta.

Ehrenreich, B. (2009) *Brightsideness: Bright-sided: How the Relentless Promotion of Positive Thinking has Undermined America.* New York: Henry Holt.

Elder-Vass, D. (2007) 'Reconciling Archer and Bourdieu in an emergentist theory of action', *Sociological Theory,* 25(4): 325–346.

Elias, N. (1991) *The Society of Individuals.* Oxford: Blackwell.

Elias, N. (2000) *The Civilizing Process: Sociogenetic and Psychogenetic Investigations.* Oxford: Blackwell.

Elias, N. and Dunning, E. (1986) *The Quest for Excitement: Sport and Leisure in the Civilizing Process.* Oxford: Basil Blackwell.

England, P. (2010) 'The gender revolution: uneven and stalled', *Gender & Society,* 24(2): 149–166.

Enwezor, O. (2001) *The Short Century: Independence and Liberation Movements in Africa, 1945–1994.* Munich, New York: Prestel.

Essed, P. (1991) *Understanding Everyday Racism: An Interdisciplinary Theory.* London and Newbury Park, CA: Sage.

Fanon, F. (1968/1961) *The Wretched of the Earth.* New York: Grove Press.

Featherstone, M (1991) 'The body in consumer culture', in M. Featherstone, M. Hepworth and B. Turner (eds) *The Body: Social Process and Cultural Theory.* London: Sage, pp 170–196.

Fenton, S. (2010) *Ethnicity.* Cambridge: Polity Press.

Ferris, K.O. (2007) 'The sociology of celebrity', *Sociology Compass,* 1(1): 371–384.

Fiske, J. and Hartley, J. (1978) *Reading Television.* London: Methuen.

Fiszbein, A., Kanbur, R. and Yemtsov, R. (2014) 'Social protection and poverty reduction: global patterns and some targets', *World Development,* 61: 167–177.

Flam, H. (2004) 'Anger in repressive regimes: a footnote to domination and the arts of resistance by James Scott', *European Journal of Social Theory,* 7(2): 171–188.

Flanagan, K. (1976) 'The sociology of pessimism', *Studies: An Irish Quarterly Review,* 65(259): 239–245.

Foster, J.B. (1999) 'Marx's theory of metabolic rift: classical foundations for environmental sociology', *American Journal of Sociology,* 105(2): 366–405.

Foucault, M. (1979) *Discipline and Punish: The Birth of the Prison.* London: Penguin.

Foucault, M. (1990a) *The History of Sexuality: Volume One. An Introduction.* London: Penguin.

Foucault, M. (1990b) *The History of Sexuality: Volume Three. The Care of the Self.* London: Penguin.

Foucault, M. (1992) *The Order of Things: An Archaeology of the Human Sciences.* London: Routledge

Franklin, A. (1999) *Animals and Modern Culture.* London: Sage.

Freire, P. (2006/1968) *Pedagogy of the Oppressed.* New York and London: Continuum.

Friedan, B. (1965) *The Feminine Mystique.* New York: Norton.

Fuchs, C. (2012) 'Social media, riots, and revolutions', *Capital & Class,* 36(3): 383–391.

Fukuyama, F. (1992) *The End of History and the Last Man.* London: Penguin.

Furlong, A. and Cartmel, F. (2007) *Young People and Social Change: New Perspectives.* Maidenhead: Open University Press.

Furlong, A., Woodman, D. and Wyn, J. (2011) 'Changing times, changing perspectives: reconciling "transition" and "cultural" perspectives on youth and young adulthood', *Journal of Sociology,* 47(4): 355–370.

Fuss, D. (1990) *Essentially Speaking: Feminism, Nature and Difference.* New York and London: Routledge.

Gabb, J. (2011) 'Family lives and relational living: taking account of otherness', *Sociological Research Online,* 16(4): 10, available at: www.socresonline.org.uk/16/4/10.html.

Gabb, J. and Fink, J. (2015) *Couple Relationships in the 21st Century.* Basingstoke: Palgrave Macmillan.

Gagnon, J. and Simon, W. ([1973] 2005) *Sexual Conduct: The Social Sources of Human Sexuality.* New Brunswick and London: Aldine Transaction.

Galeotti, M. (ed.) (2005) *Global Crime Today: The Changing Face of Organised Crime.* Abingdon: Routledge.

Game, A. and Metcalfe, S. (1996) *Passionate Sociology.* London: Sage.

Gamman, L. and Marshment, M. (eds) (1987) *The Female Gaze: Women as Viewers of Popular Culture.* London: Women's Press.

Gelles, R. J. and Harrop, J.W. (1991) 'The risk of abusive violence among children with nongenetic caretakers', *Family Relations,* 40(1): 78–83.

Geras, N. (1983) *Marx and Human Nature: Refutation of a Legend.* London: Verso.

Gerth, H.H. and Mills, C.W. (1970) 'Introduction: The man and his work', in Gerth, H.H. and Mills, C.W. (eds) *From Max Weber: Essays in Sociology.* London: Routledge and Kegan Paul.

Giddens, A. (1992) *The Transformation of Intimacy: Sexuality, Love and Eroticism in Modern Societies.* Stanford, CA: Stanford University Press.

Giddens, A. (2009) *The Politics of Climate Change*. Cambridge: Polity.

Gill, R. (2012) 'Media, empowerment and the "sexualization of culture" debates', *Sex Roles*, 66: 736–745.

Gilligan, C. (1977) 'In a different voice: women's conceptions of self and of morality', *Harvard Educational Review*, 47(4): 481–517.

Gilligan, C. (1982) *In a Different Voice: Psychological Theory and Women's Development*. Cambridge, MA: Harvard University Press.

Gimlin, D.L. (2001) *Body Work: Beauty and Self Image in American Culture*. Berkeley, CA: University of California Press.

Gladwell, M. (2010) 'Small Change: Why the Revolution Will Not be Tweeted', *New Yorker*, 4 October, available at: http://isites.harvard.edu/fs/docs/ icb.topic980025.files/Wk%2011_Nov%2011th/Gladwell_2010_Small_ Change.pdf (accessed 7 September 2015).

Glasgow University Media Group (1995) 'News talk', in J. Eldridge (ed.) *Glasgow Media Group Reader, Volume 1: News Content, Language and Visuals*. Abingdon: Routledge, pp. 170–214.

Goffman, A. (2014) *On the Run: Fugitive Life in an American City*. Chicago: University of Chicago Press.

Goffman, E. (1968) 'On the characteristics of total institutions', in *Asylums: Essays on the Social Situation of Mental Patients and Other Inmates*. Harmondsworth: Penguin, pp. 1–124.

Goffman, E. (1979) *Gender Advertisements*. London: Macmillan.

Goldstein, A. (2013) 'Big business in the BRICs', in J. Mikler (ed.) *The Handbook of Global Companies*. Chichester: Wiley-Blackwell, pp. 53–74.

González, L.A.R. (2012) 'The Mexican Movement for Peace with Justice and Dignity: An Exploratory Analysis of its Origins and Development', unpublished MA thesis. The Hague: International Institute of Social Studies.

Gouldner, A. (1970) *The Coming Crisis of Western Sociology*. New York: Basic Books.

Gradín, C. (2012) 'Poverty among minorities in the United States: explaining the racial poverty gap for blacks and latinos', *Applied Economics*, 44(29): 3793–3804.

Gramsci, A. (1973/1929) *Letters from Prison: Volume 1*. New York: Columbia University Press.

Grapendaal, M., Leuw, E. and Nelen, H. (1996) 'Legalization, decriminalization and the reduction of crime', in E. Leuw and H. Marshall (eds) *Between Prohibition and Legalization: The Dutch Experiment in Drug Policy*. Amsterdam and New York: Kugler Publications, pp 233–254.

Greco, S., Holmes, M. and McKenzie, J. (2015) 'Friendship and happiness from a sociological perspective', in M. Demir (ed.) *Friendship and Happiness: Across the Lifespan and Cultures*. New York: Springer, pp 19–35.

Green, D. and Raygorodetsky, G. (2010) 'Indigenous knowledge of a changing climate', *Climatic Change*, 100(2): 239–242.

Groenemeyer, A. (2007) 'Social problems, concept and perspectives', in G. Ritzer (ed.) *Blackwell Encyclopedia of Sociology*. Blackwell Publishing. Blackwell

Reference Online, 11 August 2011, available at: www.blackwellreference.com/subscriber/tocnode?.

Gross, N. (2005) 'The detraditionalization of intimacy reconsidered', *Sociological Theory*, 23(3): 286–311.

Grundmann, R. and Stehr, N. (2010) 'Climate change: what role for sociology?: a response to Constance Lever-Tracy', *Current Sociology*, 58(6): 897–910.

Guo, G. (2006) 'The linking of sociology and biology', *Social Forces*, 85(1): 145–149.

Guthrie, S.R. and Castelnuovo, S. (2001) 'Disability management among women with physical impairments: the contribution of physical activity', *Sociology of Sport Journal*, 18(1): 5–20

Hall, S. (1996) 'When was "the post-colonial"? Thinking at the limit', in L. Curti and I. Chambers (eds) *The Post-Colonial Question: Common Skies, Divided Horizons*. London: Routledge, pp 242–260.

Halliday, R.J. (1968) 'The sociological movement, the sociological society and the genesis of academic sociology in Britain', *Sociological Review*, 16(3): 377–398.

Halsey, A.H. (2004) *A History of Sociology in Britain*. Oxford: Oxford University Press.

Hamilton, L., Cheng, S. and Powell, B. (2007) 'Adoptive parents, adaptive parents: evaluating the importance of biological ties for parental investment', *American Sociological Review*, 72(1): 95–116.

Hammersley, M. (1999) 'Sociology, what's it for? a critique of Gouldner', *Sociological Research Online*, 4(3), available at: www.socresonline.org.uk/4/3/Hammersley.html.

Hannum, E. and Buchmann, C. (2005) 'Global educational expansion and socio-economic development: an assessment of findings from the social sciences', *World Development*, 33(3): 333–354.

Harris, A., Wyn, J. and Younes, S. (2010) 'Beyond apathetic or activist youth: 'ordinary' young people and contemporary forms of participation', *Young*, 18(1): 9–32.

Harwood-Lejeune, A. (2001). 'Rising age at marriage and fertility in Southern and Eastern Africa', *European Journal of Population*, 17(3): 261–280.

Hassan, R. (2014/2011) *Life as a Weapon: The Global Rise of Suicide Bombings*. London: Routledge.

Hennessee, J. and Nicholson, J. (1972) 'NOW says: TV commercials insult women', *New York Times Magazine*, 13: 48–51.

Hewitt, B. and De Vaus, D. (2009) 'Change in the association between premarital cohabitation and separation, Australia 1945–2000', *Journal of Marriage and Family*, 71(2): 353–361.

Higher Education Statistics Agency (2014) 'Free Online Statistics – Students & qualifiers: Sex', available at: www.hesa.ac.uk/stats (accessed 8 May 2014).

Hill, M. and Hoecker-Drysdale, S. (eds) (2001) *Harriet Martineau: Theoretical and Methodological Perspectives*. London: Routledge.

Hill-Collins, P. (1990) *Black Feminist Thought: Knowledge, Consciousness, and the Politics of Empowerment*. Boston, MA: Unwin Hyman.

Hindman, H. (2014) 'The re-enchantment of development: creating value for volunteers in Nepal', in M. Mostafanexhad and K. Hannam (eds) *Moral Encounters in Tourism*. Farnham: Ashgate, pp. 47–58.

Hlaing, K.-Y. (2012) 'Understanding recent political changes in Myanmar', *Contemporary Southeast Asia*, 34(2): 197–216.

Hobsbawm, E. and Ranger, T. (eds) (2012) *The Invention of Tradition*. Cambridge: Cambridge University Press.

Hochschild, A.R. (1973) 'A review of sex role research', *American Journal of Sociology*, 78(4): 1011–1029.

Hochschild, A.R. (2001) *The Time Bind: When Work Becomes Home and Home Becomes Work*. New York: Henry Holt.

Hochschild, A.R. (2003) *The Commercialization of Intimate Life: Notes from Home and Work*. Berkeley, CA: University of California Press.

Hochschild, A.R. and Machung, A. (2012) *The Second Shift: Working Parents and the Revolution at Home*. London: Penguin.

Holmes, M. (2004a) 'Feeling beyond rules: politicising the sociology of emotion and anger in feminist politics', *European Journal of Social Theory*, 7(2): 209–227.

Holmes, M. (2004b) 'An equal distance? Individualisation, gender and intimacy in distance relationships', *The Sociological Review*, 52(2): 180–200.

Holmes, M. (2010) 'The emotionalization of reflexivity', *Sociology*, 44(1): 139–154.

Holmes, M. (2014) *Distance Relationships: Intimacy and Emotions Amongst Academics and their Partners in Dual-Locations*. Basingstoke: Palgrave Macmillan.

Holmes, M. (2015) 'Men's emotions heteromasculinity, emotional reflexivity, and intimate relationships' *Men and Masculinities*, 18(2): 176–192.

Holmes, M. and Burrows, R. (2012) 'Ping pong poms: emotional reflexivity in return migration from Australia to the UK', *Australian Journal of Social Issues*, 47(1): 105–123.

Holmwood, J. (ed.) (2011) *A Manifesto for the Public University*. London: Bloomsbury.

hooks, b. (1992) *Black Looks: Race and Representation*. Cambridge, MA: South End Press.

Horwitz, A.V. and Wakefield, J.C. (2007) *The Loss of Sadness: How Psychiatry Transformed Normal Sorrow into Depressive Disorder*. Oxford: Oxford University Press.

Hrdy, S. (2000) *Mother Nature*. London: Vintage.

Huan, Q. (ed.) (2010) *Eco-Socialism as Politics: Rebuilding the Basis of Our Modern Civilization*. London: Springer.

Ignatow, G. (2009) 'Why the sociology of morality needs Bourdieu's habitus', *Sociological Inquiry*, 79: 98–114.

Illich, I. (1971) *Deschooling Society*. New York: Harper & Row.

Illouz, E. (1998) 'The lost innocence of love: romance as a postmodern condition', *Theory, Culture & Society*, 15(3): 161–186.

Illouz, E. (2009) 'Emotions, imagination and consumption: a new research agenda', *Journal of Consumer Culture,* 9(3): 377–413.

Imai, K., Gaiha, R. and Kang, W. (2011) 'Poverty, inequality and ethnic minorities in Vietnam', *International Review of Applied Economics,* 25(3): 249–282.

Inglis, D. (2014) 'What is worth defending in sociology today? Presentism, historical vision and the uses of sociology', *Cultural Sociology,* 8(1): 99–118.

Interparliamentary Union (2014) 'Democracy Through Partnership Between Men and Women in Politics', available at: www.ipu.org/iss-e/women.htm (accessed 3 November 2014).

Interparliamentary Union (2015) 'Women in National Parliaments', available at: www.ipu.org/wmn-e/world.htm (accessed 9 December 2015).

Irvin, G. (2008) *Super Rich: The Rise of Inequality in Britain and the United States.* Cambridge: Polity Press.

Ivana, G. (2014) 'Read Me Like an Open (Face)book'. Unpublished PhD. Universita Oberta di Barcelona.

Jackson, S. (1993) 'Even sociologists fall in love: an exploration in the sociology of emotions', *Sociology,* 27(2): 201–220.

Jackson, S. and Ho, P.S.Y. (2014) 'Mothers, daughters and sex: the negotiation of young women's sexuality in Britain and Hong Kong', *Families, Relationships and Societies,* 3(3): 387–403.

Jackson, S., Ho, P.S.Y. and Na, J.N. (2013) 'Reshaping tradition? Women negotiating the boundaries of tradition and modernity in Hong Kong and British Families', *The Sociological Review,* 61(4): 667–687.

Jackson, S. and Rees, A. (2007) 'The appalling appeal of nature: the popular influence of evolutionary psychology as a problem for sociology', *Sociology,* 41(5): 917–930.

Jaggar, A. M. (1990) 'Love and knowledge in feminist epistemology', in A.M. Jaggar and S.R. Bordo (eds) *Gender/Body/Knowledge: Feminist Reconstructions of Being and Knowing.* New Brunswick, NJ: Rutgers University Press, pp 145–171.

Jamieson, L. (1998) *Intimacy: Personal Relationships in Modern Societies.* Cambridge: Polity.

Jamieson, L. and Simpson, R. (2013) *Living Alone: Globalization, Identity and Belonging.* Basingstoke: Palgrave.

Jamieson, L., Wasoff, F. and Simpson, R. (2009) 'Solo-living, demographic and family change: the need to know more about men', *Sociological Research Online,* 14(2), available at: www.socresonline.org.uk/14/2/5.html.

Jenkins, R. (2000) 'Disenchantment, enchantment and re-enchantment: Max Weber at the millennium', *Max Weber Studies,* 1: 11–32.

Johansson, T. and Lalander, P. (2012) 'Doing resistance–youth and changing theories of resistance', *Journal of Youth Studies,* 15(8): 1078–1088.

Jones, G. W. (2007) 'Delayed marriage and very low fertility in Pacific Asia', *Population and Development Review,* 33(3): 453–478.

Jones, O. (2011) *Chavs: The Demonization of the Working Classes.* London: Verso.

Joseph, B. (2012) 'Political transition in Burma: four scenarios in the run-up to the 2015 elections', *SAIS Review of International Affairs,* 32(2): 137–149.

Kaplinksy, R. (2005) *Globalization, Poverty and Inequality*. Cambridge: Polity Press.

Karakayali, N. (2014) 'Two ontological orientations in sociology: building social ontologies and blurring the boundaries of the social', *Sociology,* 49(4): 732–747.

Kemple, T. and Mawani, R. (2009) 'The sociological imagination and its imperial shadows', *Theory, Culture & Society,* 26(7/8): 228–49.

Killian, L. (1971) 'Optimism and pessimism in sociological analysis', *The American Sociologist,* 6(4): 281–286.

King, D. S. (2006) 'Activists and emotional reflexivity: toward Touraine's subject as social movement', *Sociology,* 40(5): 873–891.

Klesse, C. (2006) 'Polyamory and its "others": contesting the terms of non-monogamy', *Sexualities,* 9(5): 565–583.

Kontula, A. (2008) 'The sex worker and her pleasure', *Current Sociology,* 56(4): 605–620.

Kotiswaran, P. (2011) *Dangerous Sex, Invisible Labor: Sex Work and the Law in India*. Princeton, NJ: Princeton University Press.

Krook, M.L. and O'Brien, D.Z. (2010) 'The politics of group representation: quotas for women and minorities worldwide', *Comparative Politics,* 42(3): 253–272.

Kumanyika, S. (2012) 'Health disparities research in global perspective: new insights and new directions', *Annual Review of Public Health,* 33: 1–5.

Kurosu, S. (2007) 'Remarriage in a stem family system in early modern Japan', *Continuity and Change,* 22(3): 429–458.

Laland, K.N. and Brown, G.R. (2011) *Sense and Nonsense: Evolutionary Perspectives on Human Behaviour*. Oxford: Oxford University Press.

Lane, R.E. (2000) *The Loss of Happiness in Market Democracies*. New Haven, CT: Yale University Press.

Lawrence, D.H. (1914) 'The shadow in the rose garden', in *The Prussian Officer and Other Stories*. London: Martin Secker, pp. 189–207.

Leahey, C., Fairchild, C. and Zarya, V. (2015) 'Women CEOs in the Fortune 500' *Fortune,* 28 October, available at: www.fortune.com/2013/05/09/women-ceos-in-the-fortune-500 (accessed 19 November 2015).

Lee, R. and Mason, A. (2014) 'Is low fertility really a problem? Population aging, dependency, and consumption', *Science,* 346(6206): 229–234.

Leibniz, G. (1952/1710) *Theodicy*. Translated by E.M. Huggard. New Haven, CT: Yale University Press.

Lever-Tracy, C. (2008) 'Global warming and sociology', *Current Sociology,* 56(3): 445–466.

Lewis, P. and Newburn, T. (2011) *Reading the Riots*. London: LSE and *The Guardian*, available at: www.guardian.co.uk/uk/series/reading-the-riots.

Lewontin, R. (1976) 'Sociobiology – a caricature of Darwin', *PSA: Proceedings of the Biennial Meeting of the Philosophy of Science Association,* 2: 22–31.

Liston, K. and Mennell, S. (2009) 'Ill met in Ghana: Jack Goody and Norbert Elias on process and progress in Africa theory', *Culture & Society,* 26(7–8): 52–70.

Loe, M. (2004) 'Sex and the senior woman: pleasure and danger in the viagra era', *Sexualities,* 7(3): 303–326.

Lu, C. (2013) 'Activist political theory and the challenge of global justice', *Ethics & Global Politics,* 6(2): 63–73.

Lyman, M.D. (2014) 'The issue of legalizing drugs', in M.D. Lyman, *Drugs in Society: Causes, Concepts and Control.* Waltham, MA: Anderson Publishing, pp. 379–402.

Mac an Ghaill, M. (1994) *The Making of Men: Masculinities, Sexualities and Schooling.* Buckingham: Open University Press.

MacPherson, C.B. (1962) *The Political Theory of Possessive Individualism: Hobbes to Locke.* Oxford: Clarendon Press.

Malhotra, V. A. (1979) 'Weber's concept of rationalization and the electronic revolution in Western classical music', *Qualitative Sociology,* 1(3): 100–120.

Malkin, C.M. and Lamb, M.E. (1994) 'Child maltreatment: a test of sociobiological theory', *Journal of Comparative Family Studies,* 25(1): 121–133.

Manning, N. (2013) '"I mainly look at things on an issue by issue basis": reflexivity and phronêsis in young people's political engagements', *Journal of Youth Studies,* 16(1): 17–33.

Manning, N. and Holmes, M. (2013) '"He's snooty 'im": white working class political dissatisfaction', *Citizenship Studies,* 17(3/4): 418–429.

Manning, N., Penfold-Mounce, R., Loader, B., Vromen, A. and Xenos, M. (2015) 'Politicians, celebrities and social media: the authenticity gap for young citizens'. Unpublished manuscript. University of York.

Martineau, H. (1838) *How to Observe Morals and Manners.* London: Charles Knight and Co. Available at http://www.aughty.org/pdf/how_observe_martineau.pdf.

Martínez, R. (2012) 'Blood and sand: making the victims visible', *Boom: A Journal of California,* 2(3): 1–4.

Marx, K. (1955/1847) *The Poverty of Philosophy.* Moscow: Progress Publishers, available at: www.marxists.org/archive/marx/works/download/pdf.htm.

Marx, K. (1959/1844) 'Estranged Labour', *Economic and Philosophical Manuscripts of 1844,* available at: www.marxists.org/archive/marx/works/1844/manuscripts/preface.htm.

Marx, K. (1969/1888) 'Theses on Feuerbach' in *Marx/Engels Selected Works, Vol. 1.* Moscow: Progress Publishers, pp. 13–15, available at: www.marxists.org/archive/marx/works/1845/theses/theses.htm.

Marx, K. (1977/1864) 'Inaugural Address of the International Working Men's Association: "The First International"', available at: www.marxists.org/archive/marx/works/1864/10/27.htm.

Marx, K. (1983/1932) 'From *The German Ideology, Volume One*', in E. Kamenka (ed.) *The Portable Karl Marx.* Harmondsworth: Penguin.

Mauthner, M. (2005) 'Distant lives, still voices: sistering in family sociology', *Sociology,* 39(4): 623–642.

May, V. (2008) 'On being a "good" mother: the moral presentation of self in written life stories', *Sociology,* 42(3): 470–486.

Mburugu, E.K. and Adams, B.N. (2005) 'Families in Kenya', in B.N. Adams and J. Trost (eds) *Handbook of World Families.* Thousand Oaks, CA: Sage, pp. 3–24.

McLennan, G. (2003) 'Sociology, Eurocentrism and postcolonial theory', *European Journal of Social Theory,* 6(1): 69–86.

McLeod, D. and Burrows, R. (2012) 'Home and away: family matters in the lives of young transnational couples', *Journal of Sociology,* 48(4): 1–15.

Mead, G.H. (1962) *Mind, Self, and Society: From the Standpoint of a Social Behaviourist.* Chicago: University of Chicago Press. First published 1934.

Miller, L. (2006) *Beauty Up: Exploring Contemporary Japanese Body Aesthetics.* Berkeley and Los Angeles, CA: University of California Press.

Miller, R. (1984) *Analyzing Marx.* Princeton, NJ: Princeton University Press.

Mills, C.W. (1943) 'The professional ideology of social pathologists', *American Journal of Sociology,* 49(2): 165–180.

Mills, C.W. (1959) *The Sociological Imagination.* New York: Oxford University Press.

Minton, T.D. (2014) 'Jails in Indian Country, 2013', *US Bureau of Justice Statistics,* available at: www.bjs.gov/index.cfm?ty=pbdetail&iid=5070 (accessed 21 November 2014).

Mol, A. and Sonnenfeld, D. (eds) (2000) *Ecological Modernisation Around the World: Perspectives and Critical Debates.* London: Frank Cass.

More, T. (1639) *The Commonwealth of Utopia: Containing a Learned and Pleasant Discourse on the Best Fate of a Public Weale, as it is Found in the Government of the New Ile Called Utopia.* London: Alsop and Fawcett.

Murphy, R. (1995) 'Sociology as if nature did not matter: an ecological critique', *British Journal of Sociology,* 46(4): 638–707.

Mutalib, H. (2012) *Singapore Malays: Being Ethnic Minority and Muslim in a Global City-State.* Abingdon and New York: Routledge.

Nadeem, S. (2009) 'Macaulay's (cyber) children: the cultural politics of outsourcing in India', *Cultural Sociology,* 3(1): 102–122.

Nielsen, F. (1994) 'Sociobiology and sociology', *Annual Review of Sociology,* 20: 267–303.

Nordman, C.J., Robilliard, A., and Roubaud, F. (2011) 'Gender and ethnic earnings gaps in seven West African cities', *Labour Economics,* 18(Supplement 1): S132–S145.

Nozaki, Y., Aranha, R., Dominguez, R.F., and Nakagima, Y. (2009) 'Gender gap and women's participation in higher education: views from Japan, Mongolia and India', in D.P. Baker and A.W. Wiseman (eds) *Gender, Equality and Education from International and Comparative Perspectives.* Bingley: Emerald Publishing, pp. 217–254.

Nussbaum, M. and Sen, A. (2004) *The Quality of Life.* New York: Routledge.

Nyong, A., Adesina, F. and Osman Elasha, B. (2007) 'The value of indigenous knowledge in climate change mitigation and adaptation strategies in the African Sahel', *Mitigation and Adaptation for Global Change,* 12(5): 787–97.

Oakley, A. (1972) *Sex, Gender and Society*. London: Temple Smith.

OECD Family Database (2014) 'SF1: Family size and household composition' and 'SF3.1: Marriage and divorce rates', OECD – Social Policy Division – Directorate of Employment, Labour and Social Affairs, available at: www.oecd.org/els/family/database.htm (accessed 2 February 2014).

Office of National Statistics (2009) 'Table 2.1: Vital Statistics Summary', *Population Trends*, 137: 63–64, (accessed 19 March 2010 at http://www.ons.gov.uk/ons/rel/population-trends-rd/population-trends/no-137-autumn-2009/population-trends.pdf).

O'Reilly, K. (2014) 'The role of the social imaginary in lifestyle migration: employing the ontology of practice theory', in M. Benson and N. Osbaldiston (eds) *Understanding Lifestyle Migration: Theoretical Approaches to Migration and the Quest for a Better Way of Life*. Basingstoke: Palgrave Macmillan, pp. 211–234.

Ostroot, N.M. and Snyder, W.W. (1985) 'Measuring cultural bias in a cross-national study', *Social Indicators Research*, 17(3): 243–251.

Owen, T. (2013) 'Towards a new sociology of genetics and human identity', *International Journal of Criminology and Sociological Theory*, 6(3): 68–80.

Owusu-Bempah, A., Kanters, S., Druyts, E., Toor, K., Muldoon, K.A., Farquhar, J.W. and Mills, E.J. (2014) 'Years of Life Lost to Incarceration: Inequities Between Aboriginal and Non-Aboriginal Canadians', *BMC Public Health*, 14(585), available at: www.biomedcentral.com/1471-2458/14/585 (accessed 21 November 2014).

Oxford English Dictionary (2006). Oxford: Oxford University Press.

Parsons, T. (1937) *The Structure of Social Action*. Glencoe, IL: Free Press.

Parsons, T. (1951) *The Social System*. London: Routledge and Kegan Paul.

Parsons, T. (1989) 'A tentative outline of American values', *Theory, Culture & Society*, 6(4): 577–612.

Parsons, T. and Bales, R.F. (1956) *Family Socialization and Interaction Process*. London: Routledge and Kegan Paul.

Parsons, T. and Shils, E.A. (eds) (2001/1951) *Toward a General Theory of Action: Theoretical Foundations for the Social Sciences*. New Brunswick, NJ: Transaction Publishers.

Pateman, C. (1988) *The Sexual Contract*. Stanford, CA: Stanford University Press.

Paxton, P., Hughes, M. M. and Painter, M. A. (2010) 'Growth in women's political representation: a longitudinal exploration of democracy, electoral system and gender quotas', *European Journal of Political Research*, 49(1): 25–52.

Peggs, K. (2013) 'The 'animal-advocacy agenda': exploring sociology for non-human animals', *Sociological Review*, 61(3): 591–606.

Pertierra, A.C. and Turner, G. (2013) *Locating Television: Zones of Consumption*. London and New York: Routledge.

Pocock, B. (2006) *The Labour Market Ate My Babies: Work, Children and a Sustainable Future*. Annandale: The Federation Press.

Popenoe, D. (2009) 'Cohabitation, marriage and child well-being: a cross-national perspective', *Society*, 46(5): 429–436.

Postone, M. and Brick, B. (1982) 'Critical pessimism and the limits of traditional Marxism', *Theory and Society,* 11(5): 617–658.

Prendergast, S. and Forrest, S. (1998) 'Shorties, low-lifers, hardnuts, and kings: boys, emotions and embodiment in schools', in G. Bendelow and S. Williams (eds) *Emotions in Social Life: Critical Themes and Contemporary Issues.* London: Routledge, pp. 155–172.

Protsyk, O. (2010) 'Promoting Inclusive Parliaments: The Representation of Minorities and Indigenous People in Parliaments, a Global Overview'. Interparliamentary Union and United Nations Development Programme.

Putnam, R.D. (2000) *Bowling Alone: The Collapse and Revival of American Community.* New York: Simon & Schuster.

Rainbird, P. (2002) 'A message for our future? The Rapa Nui (Easter Island) eco-disaster and Pacific Island environments', *World Archaeology,* 33(3): 436–451.

Rao, A.B.S.V.R. and Sekhar, K. (2002) 'Divorce: process and co-relates a cross-cultural study', *Journal of Comparative Family Studies,* 33(4): 541–563.

Reay, D., Crozier, G. and Clayton, J. (2010) '"Fitting in" or "standing out": working-class students in UK higher education', *British Educational Research Journal,* 36(1): 107–124.

Renwick, C. (2011) 'From political economy to sociology: Francis Galton and the social-scientific origin of eugenics', *British Journal for the History of Science,* 44(3): 343–369.

Renwick, C. (2012) *British Sociology's Lost Biological Roots: A History of Futures Past.* Basingstoke: Palgrave Macmillan.

Ringrose, J. (2007) 'Successful girls? Complicating post-feminist, neoliberal discourses of educational achievement and gender equality', *Gender and Education,* 19(4): 471–489.

Ritzer, G. (2010) *Enchanting a Disenchanted World: Continuity and Change in the Cathedrals of Consumption.* Thousand Oaks, CA: Pine Forge Press.

Ritzer, G. and Liska, A. (1997) '"McDisneyization" and "post-tourism": complementary perspectives on contemporary tourism', in C. Rojek and J. Urry (eds) *Touring Cultures: Transformations of Travel and Theory.* London: Routledge, pp. 96–109.

Roberts, D. and Siddiqui, S. (2015) 'Gay Marriage Declared Legal Across the US in Historic Supreme Court Ruling', *Guardian,* Friday 26 June, available at: www.theguardian.com/society/2015/jun/26/gay-marriage-legal-supreme-court (accessed 7 August 2015).

Roberts, J.V. and Melchors, R. (2003) 'The incarceration of aboriginal offenders: trends from 1978 to 2001', *Canadian Journal of Criminology and Criminal Justice,* 45(2): 211–242.

Robertson, R. and Turner, B. (1989) 'Talcott Parsons and modern social theory – an appreciation', *Theory, Culture & Society,* 6(4): 539–558.

Rojek, C. (1999) 'Abnormal leisure: invasive, mephitic and wild forms', *Leisure and Society/Loisir et Société,* 22(1): 21–37.

Rojek, C. (2000) 'Mass tourism or the re-enchantment of the world? Issues and contradictions in the study of travel', in M. Gottdiener (ed.) *New Forms of*

Consumption: Consumers, Culture and Commodification. Oxford: Rowman and Littlefield Publishers Inc., pp. 51–70.

Rollock, N., Gillborn, D., Vincent, C. and Ball, S. (2011) 'The public identities of the black middle classes: managing race in public spaces', *Sociology*, 45(6): 1078–1093.

Ronald, R. and Nakano, L. (2013) 'Single women and housing choices in urban Japan', *Gender, Place & Culture: A Journal of Feminist Geography*, 20(4): 451–469.

Rose, S., Kamin, L.J. and Lewontin, R. (1984) *Not in Our Genes: Biology, Ideology and Human Nature*. London: Pelican Books.

Roy, D. (1960) '"Banana time": job satisfaction and informal interaction', *Human Organization*, 18(4): 158–168.

Rubin, R.H. (2001) 'Alternative lifestyles revisited, or whatever happened to swingers, group marriages, and communes?', *Journal of Family Issues*, 22(6): 711–726.

Sampson, C. (2015) 'The idea of progress and indigenous peoples: Contemporary legacies of an enduring Eurocentric prophesy'. Keynote lecture to the British Sociological Association, 16th April. Glasgow Caledonian University.

Sassen, S. (2014) *Expulsions: Brutality and Complexity in the Global Economy*, Cambridge, MA and London: The Belknap Press of Harvard University.

Savage, M., Devine, F., Cunningham, N., Taylor, M., Li, Y., Hjellbrekke, J., Le Roux, B., Friedman, S. and Miles, A. (2013) 'A new model of social class? Findings from the BBC's great British class survey experiment', *Sociology*, 47(2): 219–250.

Schoen, R. and Canudas-Romo, V. (2005) 'Timing effects on first marriage: twentieth-century experience in England and Wales and the USA', *Population Studies*, 59(2): 135–146.

Selwyn, N. (2012) 'Making sense of young people, education and digital technology: the role of sociological theory', *Oxford Review of Education*, 38(1): 81–96.

Sen, A. (1987) 'Equality of what?', in S.M. MacMurrin, and M. Sterling (eds) *The Tanner Lectures on Human Values 4* (2nd edn). Cambridge: Cambridge University Press, pp. 195–220.

Sen, A. (2013) 'The ends and means of sustainability', *Journal of Human Development and Capabilities: A Multi-Disciplinary Journal for People-Centered Development*, 14(1): 6–20.

Shah, B., Dwyer, C. and Modood, T. (2010) 'Explaining educational achievement and career aspirations among young British Pakistanis: mobilizing "ethnic capital"?', *Sociology*, 44(6): 1109–1127.

Sharpe, S. (1976) *'Just Like a Girl': How Girls Learn to be Women*. Harmondsworth: Penguin.

Shilling, C. and Mellor, P.A. (1998) 'Durkheim, morality and modernity: collective effervescence, homo duplex and the sources of moral action', *The British Journal of Sociology*, 49(2): 193–209.

Shilling, C. and Mellor, P. (2010) 'Sociology and the problem of eroticism', *Sociology*, 44(3): 435–452.

Sibeon, R. (2004) *Rethinking Social Theory*. London: Sage.

Simmel, G. (1950/1908) 'The metropolis and mental life', in Kurt Wolff (Trans.) *The Sociology of Georg Simmel*. New York: Free Press, pp. 409–424.

Skeggs, B. (1997) *Formations of Class and Gender: Becoming Respectable*. London: Sage.

Skeggs, B. (2004) *Class, Self and Culture*. London: Routledge.

Skeggs, B. (2009) 'The moral economy of person production: the class relations of self-performance on "reality" television', *Sociological Review,* 57(4): 626–644.

Skelton, C. (2005) 'The 'self-interested' woman academic: a consideration of Beck's model of the "individualised individual"', *British Journal of Sociology of Education,* 26(1): 5–16.

Skelton, C. and Francis, B. (2011) 'Successful boys and literacy: are "literate boys" challenging or repackaging hegemonic masculinity?', *Curriculum Inquiry,* 41(4): 456–479.

Sklair, L. (1970) *The Sociology of Progress*. London: Routledge.

Sloterdijk, P. (2013) *You Must Change Your Life: On Anthropotechnics*. Cambridge: Polity Press.

Smart, C. (2007) *Personal Life*. Cambridge: Polity.

Smart, C. and Neale, B. (1999) *Family Fragments?* Cambridge: Polity.

Smart, C. and Shipman, B. (2004) 'Visions in monochrome: families, marriage and the individualization thesis', *British Journal of Sociology,* 55(4): 491–501.

Smith, D.E. (1987) *The Everyday World as Problematic*. Boston, MA: Northeastern University Press.

Smith, G.H. (2003) 'Indigenous struggle for the transformation of education and schooling', Keynote address to the Alaskan Federation of Natives (AFN), Anchorage, Alaska, USA, October, available at: https://faculty.washington.edu/pembina/all_articles/Smith_G2003.pdf (accessed 23 May 2014).

Sobolewska, M. (2013) 'Party strategies and the descriptive representation of ethnic minorities: the 2010 British general election', *West European Politics,* 36(3): 615–633.

Souhami, A. (2014) 'Institutional racism and police reform: an empirical critique', *Policing and Society,* 24(1): 1–21.

Spence, A. (2011) 'Labour market', *Social Trends,* 41, available at: www.ons.gov.uk/ons (accessed 9 December 2015).

Spijker, J. and MacInnes, J. (2013) 'Population ageing: the timebomb that isn't?', *British Medical Journal,* 347, available at: http://dx.doi.org/10.1136/bmj.f6598.

Spivak, G.C. (1988) 'Can the subaltern speak', in C. Nelson and D. Grossberg (eds) *Marxism and the Interpretation of Culture*. Basingstoke: Macmillan, pp. 271–313.

Standing, G. (2011) *The Precariat Charter; the Dangerous New Class*. London: Bloomsbury.

Stanley, L. and Wise, S. (1983) 'Socialization and gender role: A sort of critique', in *Breaking Out: Feminist Consciousness and Feminist Research*. London: Routledge.

Stark, R. (1999) 'Secularization, R.I.P.', *Sociology of Religion,* 60(3): 249–273.

Statistics New Zealand (2000) 'Public Prisons Service', *NZ Official Yearbook 2000,* available at: www3.stats.govt.nz/New_Zealand_Official_Yearbooks/ 2000/NZOYB_2000.html#idsect2_1_85406 (accessed 21 November 2014).

Statistics New Zealand (2014) 'New Zealand's Prison Population: The Characteristics of People in New Zealand's Prisons', *NZ Official Yearbook 2012,* available at: www.stats.govt.nz/browse_for_stats/snapshots-of-nz/ yearbook/society/crime/corrections.aspx (accessed 21 November 2014).

Stets, J.E. and Carter, M.J. (2012) 'A theory of self for the sociology of morality', *American Sociological Review,* 77(1): 120–140.

Strand, S. (2011) 'The limits of social class in explaining ethnic gaps in educational attainment', *British Educational Research Journal,* 37(2): 197–229.

Sullivan, O. (2011) 'Gender deviance neutralization through housework: where does it fit in the bigger picture? response to England, Kluwer, and Risman', *Journal of Family Theory & Review,* 3(1): 27–31.

Swyngedouw, E. (2010) 'Apocalypse forever?: Post-political populism and the spectre of climate change', *Theory, Culture and Society,* 27(2–3): 213–232.

Syed, M., Azmitia, M. and Cooper, C. R. (2011) 'Identity and academic success among underrepresented ethnic minorities: an interdisciplinary review and integration', *Journal of Social Issues,* 67(3): 442–468.

Symonds, M. and Pudsey, J. (2006) 'The forms of brotherly love in Max Weber's sociology of religion', *Sociological Theory,* 24: 133–149.

Szászy, M. (1993) 'Opening my mouth', in S. Kedgley and M. Varnham (eds) *Heading Nowhere in a Navy Blue Suit.* Wellington: Daphne Brasell Associates, pp 75–84.

Tallis, R. (1997) *Enemies of Hope: A Critique of Contemporary Pessimism.* London: Macmillan.

Tanaka, H. and Ng, C.W. (2012) 'Individualization of marriage and work life choices – a study of never-married employed women in Hong Kong and Tokyo', *Asian Women,* 28(1): 85–119.

Taylor, P. and Bain, P. (1999) '"An assembly line in the head": work and employee relations in the call centre', *Industrial Relations Journal,* 30(2): 101–117.

Therborn, G. (2004) *Between Sex and Power: Family in the World, 1900–2000.* London: Routledge.

Thin, N. (2012) *Social Happiness: Theory into Policy and Practice.* Bristol: Policy Press.

Thorat, S. and Neuman, K.S. (2012) *Blocked by Caste: Economic Discrimination in Modern India.* Oxford: Oxford University Press.

Thorne, B. (1993) *Gender Play: Girls and Boys in School.* New Brunswick, NJ: Rutgers University Press.

Tijdens, K.G. and Van Klaveren, M. (2012) 'Frozen in Time: Gender Pay Gap Unchanged for 10 Years'. Brussels: International Trade Union Confederation.

Tilly, C. (1985) 'War making and state making as organised crime', in P. Evans, D. Rueschmeyer and T. Skocpol (eds) *Bringing the State Back In.* Cambridge: Cambridge University Press, pp. 169–191.

Tokuhiro, Y. (2010) *Marriage in Contemporary Japan*. Abingdon and New York: Routledge.

Transnational Institute (2015) 'Military confrontation or political dialogue consequences of the Kokang crisis for peace and democracy in Myanmar', Transnational Institute Policy Briefing Nr. 15, 17 July, available at: www.tni. org/en/publication/military-confrontation-or-political-dialogue (accessed 28 November 2015).

Tuhiwai-Smith, L. (1999) *Decolonising Methodologies: Research and Indigenous Peoples*. London: Zed Books.

Twine, R. (2010) *Animals as Biotechnology: Ethics, Sustainability and Critical Animal Studies.* London: Earthscan.

United Nations (2013) 'World Population Prospects: The 2012 Revision', United Nations Populations Division, New York, 18 June, available at: http://data.un.org/Data.aspx?q=fertility+rates&d=PopDiv&f=variableID: 54#PopDiv (accessed 24 May 2013).

United Nations Statistics Division (2010) '"Education" in The World's Women 2010: Trends and Statistics', available at: http://unstats.un.org/unsd/ demographic/products/Worldswomen/wwEduc2010.htm (accessed 6 November 2014).

Urry, J. (2008) 'Climate change, travel and complex futures', *British Journal of Sociology,* 59(2): 261–279.

Urry, J. and Larsen, J. (2011) *The Tourist Gaze 3.0*. London: Sage. doi: http:// dx.doi.org.ezproxy.is.ed.ac.uk/10.4135/9781446251904.n4

US Bureau of Justice Statistics (2013) '"TOTAL U.S. CORRECTIONAL POPULATION DECLINED IN 2012 FOR FOURTH YEAR". Correctional Populations in the United States, 2012; Probation and Parole in the United States, 2012; and Prisoners in 2012: Trends in Admissions and Releases, 1991–2012', available at: www.bjs.gov/content/pub/press/cpus 12pr.cfm (accessed 21 November 2014).

US Department of Education (2013) 'Postsecondary and beyond: "Enrollment" and "Degrees conferred by sex and race"', *Digest of Education Statistics, 2012* (NCES (National Center for Education Statistics) 2014–15), available at: http://nces.ed.gov/fastfacts/ (accessed 10 November 2014).

Vaillancourt, J.G. (1995) 'Sociology of the environment: From human ecology to ecosociology', in M.D. Mehta and E. Ouellet (eds) *Environmental Sociology: Theory and Practice.* Canada: Captus Press, pp 3–32.

Vaillancourt, J.G. (2010) 'From environmental sociology to global sociology', in M.R. Redclift and G. Woodgate (eds) *The International Handbook of Environmental Sociology.* 2nd edn. Cheltenham: Edward Elgar, pp. 48–62.

Vaisey, S. (2007) 'Structure, culture, and community: the search for belonging in 50 urban communes', *American Sociological Review*, 72: 851–873.

Van Kriekan, R. (2012) *Celebrity Society*. London: Routledge.

Van Zoonen, L. (1995) 'Gender, representation and the media', in J. Downing, A. Mohammadi and A. Sreberny-Mohammadi (eds.) *Questioning the Media.* London: Sage, pp 311–328.

Varese, F. (2011) *Mafias on the Move: How Organized Crime Conquers New Territories*. Princeton, NJ: Princeton University Press.

Veenhoven, R. (2008) 'Sociological theories of subjective well-being', in M. Eid and R.J. Larsen (eds) *The Science of Subjective Well-Being*. New York: Guilford Press, pp. 44–61.

Veenhoven, R. (2010) 'Life is getting better: societal evolution and fit with human nature', *Social Indicators Research,* 97: 105–122.

Visser, R. and McDonald, D. (2007) 'Swings and roundabouts: management of jealousy in heterosexual "swinging" couples', *British Journal of Social Psychology,* 46(2): 459–476.

Wade, L., Sweeney, B., Derr, A.S., Messner, M.A. and Burke, C. (2014) 'Ruling Out Rape / Understanding and Ending the Campus Sexual Assault Epidemic / Drinking and Sexual Assault [Kids Just Wanna have Fun] / A Culture of Compliance vs. Prevention / Can Locker Room Rape Culture be Prevented? / Failure to Serve and Protect', *Contexts,* 13: 16–25.

Walby, S. (1996) *Gender Transformations*. London: Routledge.

Walby, S. (2013) 'Violence and society: introduction to an emerging field of sociology', *Current Sociology,* 61(2): 95–111.

Weatherburn, D. (2014) *Arresting Incarceration: Pathways Out of Indigenous Imprisonment*. Canberra: Aboriginal Studies Press.

Weber, M. (1970/1948) *From Max Weber: Essays in Sociology*. H. H. Gerth and C.W. Mills (eds). London: Routledge and Kegan Paul.

Weeks, J. (2007) '*The World We Have Won: The Remaking of Erotic and Intimate Life*. London: Routledge.

Weeks, J., Heaphy, B. and Donovan, C. (2001) *Same Sex Intimacies: Families of Choice and other Life Experiments.* London: Routledge.

Wei, C. and Qi-Yu, R. (2005) 'A study of the system of spousal maintenance on divorce: a comparison between China and Russia', *International Journal of Law, Policy and the Family,* 19(3): 310–326.

West, B. (2015) *Re-Enchanting Nationalisms: Rituals and Remembrances in a Postmodern Age*. New York: Springer-Verlag.

West, C. and Zimmerman, D. (1987) 'Doing gender', *Gender and Society,* 1(2): 125–151.

Wettergren, Å. (2009) 'Fun and laughter: culture jamming and the emotional regime of late capitalism', *Social Movement Studies,* 8(1): 1–15.

Wheaton, B. (ed.) (2004) *Understanding Lifestyle Sport: Consumption, Identity and Difference*. London: Routledge.

Wilding, R. (2006) '"Virtual" intimacies? Families communicating across transnational contexts', *Global Networks,* 6(2): 125–142.

Wilkie, R. (2010) *Livestock/Deadstock: Working with Farm Animals from Birth to Slaughter*. Philadelphia, PA: Temple University Press.

Wilkie, R. (2015) 'Multispecies scholarship and encounters: changing assumptions at the human–animal nexus', *Sociology,* 49(2): 323–339.

Wilkie, R. and McKinnon, A. (2013) 'George Herbert Mead on humans and other animals: social relations after human–animal studies', *Sociological*

Research Online, 18(4): 19, available at: www.socresonline.org.uk/18/4/19. html 10.5153/sro.3191.

Wilkinson, R. and Pickett, K. (2009) *The Spirit Level: Why Equality is Good for Everyone.* London: Penguin.

Williams, J. (2002) *Eyes on the Prize: America's Civil Rights Years, 1954–1965.* New York and London: Penguin.

Williamson, J. (1978) *Decoding Advertisements: Ideology and Meaning in Advertising.* London: Marion Boyars.

Willis, P. (1977) *Learning to Labour: How Working Class Kids Get Working Class Jobs.* Farnborough: Saxon House.

Wilson, B. (2009) 'Estimating the cohabiting population', *Population Trends,* 136: 21–27.

Wilson, E.O. (1975) *Sociobiology: The New Synthesis.* Cambridge, MA: Harvard University Press.

Wing Lo, T. (2010) 'Beyond social capital: triad organized crime in Hong Kong and China', *British Journal of Criminology,* 50(5): 851–872.

Wood, A.W. (1981) *Karl Marx.* Boston: Routledge and Kegan Paul.

Wood, H. and Skeggs, B. (eds) (2011) *Reality Television and Class.* Basingstoke: Palgrave Macmillan.

Woolf, V. (1986/1938) *Three Guineas.* London: Hogarth Press.

Woollacott, A. (2006) *Gender and Empire.* Basingstoke: Palgrave Macmillan.

World Bank (2012) *World Development Indicators 2012.* World Bank Publications.

World Bank (2016) 'Data: GDP (current US$)', available at: http://data. worldbank.org/indicator/NY.GDP.MKTP.CD (accessed 26 January 2016).

World Health Organization (2013) 'Violence against women: Intimate partner and sexual violence against women' Fact sheet N^0 239, October, available at: www.who.int/mediacentre/factsheets/fs239/en/ (accessed 17 July 2014).

Wouters, C. (2007) *Informalization: Manners and Emotions Since 1890.* London: Sage.

Wright, E. O. (2010) *Envisioning Real Utopias.* London: Verso.

Wyn, J. (2012) 'Peer groups', in N. Lesko and S. Talbot (eds) *Keywords in Youth Studies: Tracing Affects, Movements, Knowledges.* New York: Routledge, pp. 92–97.

Young, A. (2014) 'Cities in the city: street art, enchantment, and the urban commons', *Law & Literature,* 26(2): 145–161.

Young, I.M. (1991) *Justice and the Politics of Difference.* Princeton, NJ: Princeton University Press.

YWCA Scotland (2016) *YWCA Scotland: Young Women's Movement.* www. ywcascotland.org

Yuval-Davis, N. (2006) 'Intersectionality and feminist politics', *European Journal of Women's Studies,* 13(3): 193–209.

Zureick-Brown, S., Newby, H., Chou, D., Mizoguchi, N., Say, L., Suzuki, E. and Wilmoth, J. (2013) 'Understanding global trends in maternal mortality', *International Perspectives on Sexual & Reproductive Health,* 39(1): 32–41.

INDEX